I ♥ HAPPY CATS

Thank you

To all cat lovers and their cats who, over the years, have provided me with the insights I can now share with the wider world. Together, we keep cats out of the shelter.

To my sister Jolien and my mother Kristel, who have always supported me in every crazy idea I've ever had, including this book :) Without you, Felinova could never have grown like this! To my father Jan, whose wise council and deep insights never leave me unmoved.

To my mentor Anne McBride, from whom i've learned to keep challenging everything i know.

To everyone who believed in this book, *you know who you are!*

To Astrid, my best friend and outstanding design artist, for the book's beautiful design and the lovely moral support ;)

To Nicky, Zoe & Bizzy who are a constant inspiration and support, thanks for falling in love with this 'baby' ;)

To Bence, for the beautiful illustrations and to Andrew and his cat Whisky for the English translation.

To my cat coaches for the eternal support and passion to fight for happier cats.

To everyone who believes in and continues to believe in me and Felinova.

With love, Anneleen

Colophon

Anneleen Bru
Felinova Comm. V
Broekdam-Noord 45a
9150 Kruibeke
Belgium
anneleen@felinova.be

www.ilovehappycats.com

First print: May 2018

ISBN : 9789082772227
EAN : 9789082772227
Legal file number: D/2018/14.325/2

Credits

Design: Astrid Vanderborght
www.astrid.graphics
Illustrator: Bence Berszán Árus
Translator: Andrew Mitchell

Photos: www.unsplash.com

Photographers: Erica Leong p.12
Kari Shea p.18
Simone Dalmeri p.26
Chaiyaporn Atakampeewong p.50
Kari Shea p.54
Chang Duong p.60
Mohamed Nohassi p.82
Alejandra Coral p.98
Shubhankar Sharma p.108
Paul Hanaoko p.128
Erik-Jan Leusink p.132
Ahmed Saffu p.142
Koen Eijkdenboom p.152
Jerzy Dubovitsky p.156
Michal Grosicki p.168
Max Belttinger p.174
Sarah Dorweiler p.180
Marko Blazevic p.190
Jonas Vincent p.196
Paul Hanaoko p.202
Mikhail Vasilyev p.208
Sabri Tuzcu p.214

For more information and bookings, visit us at www.ilovehappycats.com or contact me at anneleen@felinova.be. We'd love to hear from you!

What will you find in this book?

First things first.

Having a cat in your home is a tremendous privilege and the charisma of cats is irresistible.

This book is for every cat lover - whether you work with cats on a daily basis or have a couple of sweet kitties at home. Whether you've been caught by the cat bug for years or have only just adopted a kitten, this book will inspire you to better understand your cat and make small adaptations in your home and your own behaviour that will see your cat become happier every day.

Because optimal harmony between cats and their owners leads to greater well-being, happier owners, and fewer cats in animal shelters.
As a behavioural therapist for cats, I have had hundreds of consultations with owners whose cats were displaying undesirable behaviour. These problems are often caused by misunderstandings and because people tend to interpret the cat's behaviour from a human perspective.

Over the years, many different and interesting patterns arose, which I would like to share with you.
Solving and improving this undesired behaviour generates insight into how it could have been prevented.

This book is a culmination of insights and tips that we have tried and approved over the years.

On the one hand, the aim of this book is to better understand cat behaviour by explaining the theory behind their behaviour, thereby improving their well-being. On the other hand, we want to increase your pleasure as a cat owner by providing practical tips that will make your cat happier and improve the relationship you share together.

This therefore is a book filled with useful and practical tips based on scientific info and years of experience that will make your cat happier. Allow yourself to be inspired, but don't be discouraged. There's no need to do everything in this book (straight away) :).

In relation to the advice I give as a therapist, I think it's important that the tips are realistic and affordable, and that you are able to see changes in your cat's behaviour within four to six weeks.

You probably already have a happy cat, but with our advice and tips, your cat could become even happier.

Maybe you've been observing tension between your cats, or you're not sure whether your cat is really happy. In this book, you will undoubtedly find a wealth of new insights on what drives your mysterious little tiger.

There are many different opinions and philosophies concerning cats and their behaviour, and that's perfectly alright (although some insights are more scientifically supported than others). We always try to always remain respectful towards the choices people make, their budgets, motivation and their available time. This book will assist you to make better supported choices and to feel more confident about how you treat your cat and meet its needs.

Whatever your feelings are while reading this book, follow your gut instinct. You know your cat best. If your gut instinct tells you an instruction in this book won't work for your cat, or, if after trying something out, you conclude things were better before, follow your instincts!

As a final note before we get started. While the aim of this book is to optimise your cat's life, we must make sure to implement changes in a calm manner. That's why we only ask you to only 'add' modifications at home, so don't suddenly start removing and replacing things! This can be very alarming for your cat. Do you want to experiment? Leave everything the way it was and only add things to other locations. Use the upcoming weeks to find out what works, and then gradually remove those items that are no longer being used. Don't go through your house in a whirlwind. Instead, implement changes slowly.

Have fun reading this book! And I promise you that your relationship with your cat will never be the same again.

Anneleen Bru

MSc in Companion Animal Behaviour Counselling

(University of Southampton, UK)

Behavioural therapist for cats

Felinova Animal Behaviour Consulting

CRAZY
CAT LADIES
ARE OUT,
HAPPY CAT
LADIES ARE IN!

#happycatlady
#ilovehappycats

Let's do this!

What
do you
really
have at
home?

"Your domestic cat
is programmed
identically to
its ancestors.
So brace yourself."
Anneleen Bru

BACKGROUND CHECK OF YOUR CAT

Felis sylvestris... come again?

The domestic cat is descended from the African wildcat *(Felis sylvestris lybica)*. We know this through extensive research into their DNA and behaviour. Our cat's ancestor inhabits North Africa and the Middle East and is a highly territorial, solitary and opportunistic hunter with quite a repertoire of quirks and unusual habits.

Like any successful hunter, this wild cat developed a specific range of communication forms, ways of dealing with conflicts, hunting skills and behaviours that are adapted to life in various habitats (steppe, savannah, forest, desert) and varying conditions and circumstances.

However, the African wildcat also has its limitations. Most notably, it has difficulty dealing with other cats, because it did not evolve in a group and its adaptive capacity falls short in this area. This has in part resulted in the fact that as members of the *Felis sylvestris lybica* family, cats are incredibly sensitive to stress.

It is important to know that, sharing the same instincts, needs, preferences and expectations, your domestic cat and its ancestor are like two peas in a pod. So, whether your cat is a British Shorthair, a blue-eyed Birman or a fabulous shelter cat, it has the same basic programming.

The (self-)domestication of the domestic cat is a fairly recent process, in which the cat has gradually traded its rugged, solitary existence with few resources for an abundance of food.

In exchange, the cat must adopt a tolerant attitude towards other cats and people. And this is perfectly possible, albeit with variations among individuals.

In fact, if all environmental factors are optimal, cats can even establish strong social ties with other cats.

Curriculum vitae of the African wildcat

- Highly territorial animal
- Solitary hunter
- Shy character, prone to hiding
- Victim to larger predators
- Only has social contact during mating season
- Quickly adapts to its environment
- Predominantly active at night time and during dusk and dawn
- Avoids conflict, protects itself by running away
- Eats small prey multiple times a day
- Hunts mice, birds, insects, reptiles and amphibians
- Drinking is not a priority due to the high moisture content in its prey
- Highly vulnerable as solitary hunters, so don't display pain

The hereditary characteristics that our domestic cat has inherited from its ancestors express themselves in small, subtle behaviour that often appears strange to people, but is often heavily programmed, even though they may no longer seem relevant to us.

A few examples are:

- Deeply burying excrement in the litter tray, because these smells could attract predators.
- Scraping around the bowl to 'bury' biscuits for the same reason.
- Staring at enemies
- Experiencing other, unknown cats as hostile
- Eating small meals an average of 10 to 20 times a day
- Feeling highly vulnerable while drinking and visiting the litter tray
- Possessing a highly limited repertoire of social signals towards other cats
- No social reconciliatory behaviour towards each other; in the desert, cats would simply retreat.
- Working through certain daily routines to keep their habitat recognisable by releasing pheromones
- Prone to stress due to changes and new or unfamiliar things
- Bringing themselves to safety
- Not displaying pain

Preferences they've inherited from their great-uncle *Lybica*:

- Soft sand to do their business in, like in the desert
- High positions to keep watch from and to bring themselves to safety
- Soft, malleable surfaces, like wood and bark, to put their nails in
- Moving prey instead of stationary prey
- Flowing water instead of stagnant water
- Large surfaces to eat and drink from, so that their whiskers don't touch anything
- Small spaces to hide in

"Understanding
your cats starts
with realising how
differently from us
they see, feel, hear
and smell the world."
Anneleen Bru

HOW YOUR CAT PERCEIVES THE WORLD

Your cat doesn't see what you see

Cats have sharper vision than humans, but they see fewer colours. We have one cone on our retina (to perceive colour) and four rods (to perceive the difference between light and dark; in other words, sharpness). Cats have one cone versus twenty rods, allowing them to see even the smallest movements in the distance. This is highly efficient for their chances of survival and to catch prey.

Cats perceive blue, green, and a little bit of yellow. Colours like red, pink, brown and orange are like different shades of grey to them. They also distinguish between more shades of grey than humans. Therefore, the colour of a prey is not at all relevant to them.

Instead, movements, sounds and smells are very important to them. What does play a role for cats is the contrast between an object or prey and the surface. If you have a light floor, it's best to use dark toys. If you have a dark floor, it's better to use light toys.

Cats can also see incredibly well in the dark and only need one sixth of the amount of light humans need to see. They also have a reflective layer behind their eyeball (the tapetum lucidum) that reflects even the smallest glimmers of light. Thus, their eyes do need a bit of light. Cats are also unable to see in complete darkness.

Cats can only sharply see objects that are at least one metre removed from their noses. They cannot focus on objects that are closer, instead using their whiskers and legs to measure things like distance, location and mobility. This means that many owners do not play with their cats in the most suitable way when they dangle their toys right in front of their noses. The cat merely experiences a fuzzy image and, as a result, isn't triggered to really play with the object.

Sometimes, owners incorrectly reach the conclusion that their cat doesn't like to play, which is a shame, because they do. Cats prefer to follow something moving away from them at a distance of a few metres. This triggers their hunting instinct!

FACT - Do you remember those YouTube videos in which cucumbers were placed behind eating cats, causing them to jump out of their skin? As professionals, they were very hard for us to watch, because the cucumbers scared them to death. Myself and colleagues around the globe immediately called upon cat owners NOT to do this, however funny it may seem. This is because the cat is safely eating in its core area (more about this later), which it expects to be entirely predictable. Cats don't see clearly at less than a metre, so these cucumbers were simply large, unclear objects creeping up on them, ready to strike. Your cat isn't merely frightened once, but instead learns that its core area is no longer safe. This stimulates behaviours like fear, spraying and generally restless behaviour. So don't do it!

Recent studies have shown us that it is highly likely that cats can also perceive vision in ultraviolet. Quite interesting if you consider that cats can secrete pheromones and scent trails in their environment, often paired with urine, like with spraying. It could therefore be the case that the animals not only give off a scent signal, but also secrete a colour, thereby further enhancing the effect of the signal.

You cannot hear what your cat hears

The hearing of a cat is fine-tuned to detect prey. People hear sounds between 5 and 20 kHz, depending on their age. Cats can perceive sounds up to 60 kHz, which is an important fact. Consider all those electronic devices that are active in and around your house and which generate inaudible sounds to us, but are clearly audible to them. Because of this, in therapy sessions, I sometimes ask people to unplug all devices to see if there is a change in the cat's behaviour. This is because electrical noise can have an incredibly overstimulating effect on some cats, causing them to become frustrated and/or stressed. Although cats can hear more wavelengths than us, this does not mean cats hear the sounds we hear more strongly. They are simply capable of perceiving a wider range of frequencies.

Cats not only perceive the strength of sounds, but also their pitch and depth. They can determine whether sounds are close to each other or not, while also distinguishing between sounds close to each other. This is because it is vital for cats to detect small prey and hear danger coming.

Colours do not matter to cats

Walk into an average pet shop and you are overwhelmed with cat toys in all shapes and colours. However, these colours are not at all important for your cat. The shape could play a role, as well as the material from which a toy is made. What cats also think is very important is how prey animals or toys smell, sound (fluttering, chirping) and move.

Therefore, pretty colours are irrelevant and are mostly there to attract people and to stimulate us to buy the nice toys. You should, as previously mentioned, consider the contrast between the toy and the surface on which the cat will be playing with it.

The fur, oh so sensitive

Your cat has highly sensitive fur, with a host of receptors that respond to touch, pressure, movement, pain and temperature. As solitary hunters, cats do not have a lot of physical contact with other cats and predominantly use their fur to obtain information from their environment.

A cat's fur is so sensitive that a single rub or stroke on a spot is the human equivalent of 20 hard scratches on that same spot. Not so sweet and soft then, but rather, painful and annoying.

The phenomenon of stroking, therefore, is not something cats inherently enjoy, unless they were accustomed to it at an early age (between two and seven weeks), preferably while suckling from their mother, since this creates a positive association. We will return to this later on in the book.

Cuddling and stroking is something we as people do consider important as they are human ways of showing affection. It is best to adapt our expectations towards as our cats, as well how we stroke them. Stick to a few strokes, preferably on the head, and then stop. Does the cat itself ask for more? Then you can stroke again, but always stroke in blocks of no more than two or three strokes.

And this is how we arrive at stories of 'mean cats'. If by now we understand that as solitary hunters cats do not have many ways of saying 'stop' or 'enough', they will need to quickly switch to clear signals (like biting, scratching or striking) to indicate that you have stroked them enough and it's time for you to stop.

The whiskers, more important than you might think

Have you ever properly looked at your cat's whiskers? They're not just an excellent part of the cat's body for a person to see how it's feeling, but also an important tool to use to collect information. A cat's whiskers are thin towards their tips and become thicker closer to the skin.

Cats use them to locate prey at distance of less than a metre, because they only have blurry vision within that area, remember?

Thus, whiskers are antennae, and so sensitive that they can pass on quite a bit of information to the muscles they're connected to. Those muscles are in direct contact with the brain. And in this way, despite its blurry vision at short distances, cats can still locate their prey exceptionally well, and respond extraordinarily quickly to any small movement.

Cats also use their whiskers to detect whether their prey still has a pulse. On top of that, they can absorb and secrete smells more easily through their whiskers.

Additionally, they also use their feelers to check whether their entire body will fit through an opening. If their whiskers don't touch the edges of a gap they want to fit through, then they will fit through entirely.

"No two cats
are the same,
and we must respect that
if we want to make
them happy"
Anneleen Bru

INDIVIDUAL DIFFERENCES IN BEHAVIOUR

Cat personalities?

Cats display individual differences in their behaviour. And however much we would like to speak of cat 'personalities', it is nearly impossible. This is because having a personality means a certain living being will display fixed, consistent behaviour over time and in different situations, despite varying influences.

With cats, there are too many external influences affecting their behaviour to effectively speak of consistent behaviour.

What is more interesting when trying to determine your cat's character is to see which influences cause your current cat to behave differently than your previous cat would have in the same situation, or which factors cause your cat to behave differently in different circumstances.

During consultations, owners often say things like 'my previous cats never did that', 'my previous cat never had a problem with that' or 'my parent's cat would have responded differently to that'.

So why is that?

In this chapter we will look at the different influences on the behaviour of your cat!

Your cat's character has two factors

Your cat's character is determined by two important factors. On the basis of these two factors, four combinations can be made to describe a cat's behaviour. The two factors will be supplemented later on with broad influences on cat behaviour.

Dominant? No! Confident!

Factor 1 is the innate level of your cat's confidence, also often misunderstood as 'dominance' or 'submissiveness'. Dominance doesn't exist among cats, since they are inherently solitary hunters and don't need a fixed hierarchy to survive.

A cat's confidence level is innate and has different levels, ranging from very shy to very confident. This innate trait largely determines how cats deal with their environment.

When a shy cat feels threatened, it will retreat and hide in a high or safe place, such as the attic. This type of insecure cat will be less likely to spray when stressed. They prefer to keep as quiet as possible, so that they don't attract attention.

A confident cat, on the other hand, will not hold back from displaying aggressive behaviour, like striking out and attacking when afraid or frustrated. Nor do these cats make it a secret when they don't feel good, because they start spraying.

Shy cats have smaller territories and are more careful by being less curious and less prominent.

Confident cats are much more curious and generally feel more like exploring - a larger territory is often the logical consequence.

Socialisation during the first seven weeks

Factor 2 is socialisation. A cat is always socialised with respect to something, namely the environment and the living creatures it was familiarised with during the first seven weeks of its life.

Scientifically, the socialisation period has been more exactly determined as the period between two and seven weeks. Within this period, cats learn about all the things that are normal and what should or shouldn't frighten them.

Cats learn this by being exposed to different stimuli in a non-invasive or non-intense way, in which the animals are consistently given the opportunity to investigate, but also to leave should they want to. At this age, kittens don't have an automatic fright response, which means they will not automatically perceive everything as threatening.

If a young cat grew up on a farm, it will feel most comfortable in a similar environment at a later age.

If a cat grew up around people who were actively working on socialising kittens and letting them get used to all kinds of stimuli from the human world, then the cat will feel best in an environment surrounded by people.

And now?

Both factors (degree of confidence and socialisation) are therefore not only ways to explain your cat's behaviour, but also tools to find out how to improve your cat's well-being.

By selecting adoptees based on their socialisation, for example, and training animals to become familiar with certain things in the environment of their new home (repeatedly, if necessary), you increase the chance of success of an adoption, and the successful well-being of cat and owner. In which 'category' your cat belongs is certainly not binding and final forever. For example, in adapted situations, shy cats can bloom and become more confident. Sadly, the opposite can also be true.

With the right kind of patience and suitable training techniques, cats that aren't entirely socialised can feel better in the environment in which they have to live, even if they weren't fully socialised to it at an early age.

Therefore, when introducing a cat into your home, it is best to find out where the animal is from, how it was raised in the first weeks and where it grew up.

Confident and properly socialised

The cat has a lot of confidence and was also socialised to the environment it currently lives in as a kitten.
It explores to its heart's content and isn't frightened easily because it knows everything. These cats are first on the scene and aren't afraid to intimidate other cats or block the path to their resources (food, drink, toys, ...) to keep them to themselves.
This scenario is most likely to lead to a happy cat. But it is not always ideal if there are other, shyer cats living in the same house.

Not confident and not properly socialised

This cat is very shy and is incredibly susceptible to matters and events in its environment. The cat is frightened easily because there are many things it isn't familiar with and it never learnt that those things are okay. These cats suffer most from stressful situations, because they find stimuli and experiences threatening. These cats then pull back, changing nothing about their situation as a result.
Since due to this behaviour they don't learn anything new, nothing changes for them. Therefore, it is best to place these cats in an environment similar to the one in which they grew up.

Confident and not properly socialised

The cat has a lot of confidence, but isn't socialised to the environment it is in. As a consequence, it is often frightened by situations in its surroundings, because it isn't familiar with them and experiences them as threatening. These cats will clearly display their fear through aggression, fearful behaviour, or clear communication tools like scratching and spraying. This type of cat therefore is actively responsive to its environment. As a result, its confident character does give the cat an outlet to deal with its emotions, because the animal can actually change something about the situation it finds itself in. The cat could, for example, chase away enemies and secrete scent signals that enhance the predictability of its territory. These cats will approach you and tolerate limited moments of stroking, but will rarely sit on your lap, instead lying next to or nearby you.

Not confident and properly socialised

This cat is shy, but properly socialised to its environment. The cat doesn't have many fright responses, but will often view things from a distance first before exploring them. These cats love to have contact with you, but will be timid around visitors.

Influences on your cat's behaviour

In addition to the previous four combinations, there are numerous other possible influences on your cat's behaviour, determining why your cat responds in a certain way and not like your neighbour's cat or your previous cat.

However, it isn't an exact science, and the characteristics or combinations are never final, nor are they always applicable for all cats in all situations. This is because it's often about a mix of all kinds of influences.

Therefore, don't 'pigeonhole' your cat by placing your cat in one of the categories according to the two factors, but rather, use the factors as necessary background information and as possible explanations of why your cat is more likely to or not to display certain behaviour towards you and other cats. This leads to greater insight and understanding.

Genetic background

From scientific studies we know that the character of a cat's father influences the cat's confidence. Multiple studies have shown that kittens of confident fathers also have more confidence, socialising to their environment faster and becoming friendlier as a result.

Prenatal influences

Mother cats that are exposed to stress during pregnancy, and as a result have higher cortisol levels in the blood, have more reactive kittens.

These are kittens that will respond fearfully more quickly, and which will often see things as threats. Unsurprisingly, having been born in times of stress and danger, these cats need to respond to threats quickly and efficiently.

Fur colours

We used to think that there was a relationship between the colour of a cat's fur and its behaviour. Cats with a creamy or ginger fur colour were supposed to be more aggressive and less tolerant towards people they didn't know, and more temperamental.

In the meantime, however, the existing scientific studies have been called into question, and we assume that there is no reliable, final scientific research that indicates that certain colours consistently result in certain characteristics among cats.

Further studies into the perception of characteristics of different colours of cats among cat owners further showed that there is a relationship between different colours (white, black, two colours, three colours and ginger) and traits like distant, friendly, intolerant, calm and shy. Of course, this only concerns the perceptions of cat owners, and not effective relationships among the cats themselves.

In any case, colour is only one small box in the large repertoire of possible influences on the behaviour of cats. We should therefore not dwell on it for too long.

Breed

Cat breeds are not just described based on their morphological or outward characteristics; they can also be divided based on their specific behaviours. Particular links can certainly be made, although we don't have decisive scientific proof to support these connections.

As such, Bengals are supposed to very energetic. Eastern breeds, like the Siamese or Balinese, are very active, vocal and social, and have a greater chance of displaying pica (the eating of non-edible things, like fabrics, for example). Ragdolls are bred for traits like docile and affection, like real dolls. Birmans are more independent, but are very sociable. Russian Blues are supposed to be shyer and Persians have a greater chance of displaying behavioural problems. Of course, as therapists, we take this into account, but it is never the decisive reason or cause of a certain behaviour or problem.

As such, it is not a good idea to have different expectations of pedigree cats than of average domestic cats. Regardless of whether your cat has white fur and blue eyes, a tabby coat and a flat nose, special stripes or any other pattern, all cats are programmed in the same way and have the same needs and instincts.

People, for example, often expect that pedigree cats can be kept in an apartment without causing problems, because of their higher purchase price, the fear that they will be stolen, or that they have fewer cat skills to survive outdoor life. Nothing could be further from the truth. Pedigree cats may not know the outside world, but these cats have the same need to explore, hunt and climb as any ordinary street or shelter cat.

Environment

The environment a cat lives in has a large influence on how it behaves. Consequentially, cats are very attached to their environment! This is why it is best to leave cats at home as much as possible. Putting cats in different spaces is not only incredibly stressful for them, the change will also elicit behaviour other than that which the animal displays in its trusted environment, due to a host of environmental influences (sounds, smells, new things, etc.).

Whether the environment adequately plays into the needs and natural instincts of the cat will also influence its behaviour to both people and other cats. Whether the cat can adopt a tolerant attitude or feels safe therefore depends on what the environment provides in terms of eating places, drinking resources, litter trays, hiding places, scratching places, hunting opportunities and food enrichment.

We know that the largest stress factor among cats is not the presence or absence of a threat, but rather the options and choices the cat has within its environment to deal with potential threats. Can the animal retreat to a safe place and be left alone? Are the necessary resources (food, drink, litter trays, etc.) predictable and freely accessible? Cats are opportunists through and through and like to be in control!

If cats are given sufficient choice to decide where they can feel safe depending on the danger, they will generally feel much better. The supply of resources, the tools to deal with stress and enrichment in the environment therefore have a decisive influence on the cat's daily behaviour and well-being, and how its positions itself towards other cats and people.

Individual preferences

Your cat isn't only born with an individual character in terms of confidence, it also develops its own preferences after birth and as a result of its socialisation.

These preferences express themselves in, for example, the locations of resources, prey smells that excite them, where they like to be stroked, which voices and people they find more pleasant, in what kind of place they like to sleep, or whether they prefer to sit on the floor or up high, and so on.

These individual preferences can change throughout the cat's life and are the main reason why in this book we will speak of the principle of installing a 'supermarket' in the living environment of the cat, so that your cat, with all its preferences, can choose and decide for itself.

Learned behaviour

Any animal that lives for more than two seasons learns. Every day, for example, it learns which signals in the environment indicate good things and which announce something negative. With animal species, their intelligence is linked to this; namely, how quickly does the animal create associations in its environment. Cats are no different; every day, they learn what behaviour leads to which results.

As previously mentioned, cats are opportunists, and will use every opportunity to get something (preferably without too much effort) that is important to them, like food, attention, access to outside, something new to explore, and so on.

This opportunistic behaviour has made cats into incredibly cunning, intelligent animals that know precisely in which situation, with which person, at what hour of the day, in which circumstances, in which room, during which activity and even during which of their owner's moods they can get exactly what they want.

Cats walk around all day observing their habitats, with us as owners in that habitat. They know which movements you make in bed when you're almost getting up, they know that the alarm means you are getting up and will feed them, and they know quite well that when the phone rings, they won't be getting any attention.

Be aware of this; your cat is very clever and you can teach it many new things if you want to. People often say or think that you cannot teach cats anything, saying things like 'they aren't as clever as dogs'. Well, cats are at least as clever as dogs. They are simply harder to motivate.

That trait is important for us, because it means that we are perfectly able to change unwanted behaviour among cats. This is because cats continue to learn (new) things. They will not forget what happened previously, but create new associations every day.

Thus, a cat's behaviour will not depend solely on what is happening at a certain time, but is also influenced by all previous, comparable situations in the past and in what way and how successfully the cat was able to respond to them at the time.

FACT - There are no 'mean' cats. Cats with behaviour that is sometimes described as being mean are animals that have learnt that they cannot achieve anything with other, clear communication forms and stress signals. In the past, they learnt that subtle ways to communicate that something isn't alright are of no use, as the people or other cats around them did not see or understand these signals.
Now, they immediately switch to the clearest and most successful strategy, which they're sure it will work. This is why there are cats that bite or strike out straight away, instead of first hissing or arching their backs.

EMOTIONS & MOTIVATIONS

Motivations & emotions

Cats have good reasons for doing what they do. It's that simple. When your cat does something, you may wonder: 'Why does it do that?'

In any case, the reasons cats do something are very logical to them, and usually have almost nothing to do with us, but rather, with their way of 'surviving'.

In addition to their degree of confidence, socialisation and the influences of their behaviour, the internal emotional life of your cat also influences its daily behaviour. This expresses itself in motivations (what the cat wants) and emotions (their associated drives).

Two important parts to further understand what drives your cat to do what it does:

Motivations

Cats are inherently sensitive to stress, but what exactly is important for them to experience no stress or as little stress as possible? What moves, drives and motivates the cat and to which factors in its environment will it respond?

We assume that all animals do what they do due to the five following reasons that motivate them to display certain behaviours:

1. Food

A cat won't survive without food. Therefore, food is the most important drive for its behaviour. A cat will even put itself in unsafe situations to obtain food, although naturally it would prefer to be able to eat in a safe location and according to a natural pattern. But if the situation isn't ideal, these preferences may vary. Food above all else!

2. Safety

As solitary hunters, it is important that cats are able to bring themselves to safety and are continuously ready to deal with potential sources of danger in their environment. The danger of a larger or unknown predator is always lurking just around the corner.

3. Reproduction

Like all animals, cats are tremendously driven to procreate, which explains a great deal of their behaviour in terms of communication, roaming and aggression. However, this motivation is less important to us, because we have all our cats neutered. This does not mean that roaming outdoor cats no longer have an influence on their behaviour.

4. Obtaining nice things

Cats want to get the nice things in life that aren't essential for survival in themselves, like attention, treats, outdoor access, toys, and so on.

5. Avoiding unpleasant things

Cats want to avoid unpleasant matters, even if they aren't life threatening, like not being able to go outside, not getting a treat or attention, owners not waking up on time, and so on.

Emotions

Every animal has its basic emotions as drives to achieve the above-mentioned motivations necessary for life. Feeling a certain emotion guides the internal system to undertake a particular action. Therefore, if we want to analyse behaviour, it is important to look at the underlying emotion. This provides us with a clearer view of a potential solution for problematic behaviour.

Aggression, for example, often occurs as a consequence of emotions of fear, anxiety, frustration or pleasure. Solving an aggression problem requires a different approach for each of these emotions.

Although we do not know everything about emotions among animals, we can certainly speak of the following strong basic emotions among cats, that will lead to particular behaviour being shown more or less in future.

These basic emotions (fear, frustration, pleasure, relief) lie primarily at the root of cat behaviour. In other words, the emotions a cat feels when something is effectively happening or immediately after it has happened. There can also be 'predictive' emotions, like anxiety and anticipation, at the heart of cat behaviour, wherein the animal will already feel a similar feeling when experiencing reliable, predictive signals in its environment that could point towards something about to happen that could potentially or will generate these basic emotions.

1. Fear

The feeling you get when there's a large predator right in front you. This emotion causes responses like fleeing, fighting, fiddling about or freezing to get out of the way of the trigger.

2. Frustration

The feeling you get when the world doesn't do what you expect it to do. This is an incredibly strong emotion that leads to a host of responses to stop that feeling.

3. Anxiety

The feeling you get if experience has taught you that something is about to happen that could possible cause you to feel frustration or fear. Although the presence of an effective stress factor might be missing, this feeling is often almost as strong as if it were present. Anxiety is a problem among cats that should not be underestimated. With anxiety, it is not only necessary to remove the stress factor itself, but also to create a new positive association with all signals in the environment that previously predicted the stress factor.

4. Pleasure

The feeling you get if you get/have something that gives you a nice feeling, both physically and mentally. This is something you want to pursue, and the behaviour that generates this emotion will increase.

5. Relief

The feeling you get when you've managed to avoid something unpleasant. These behaviours will also increase.

6. Anticipation

The feeling you get when you expect something nice to happen without it being effectively present. For cats, think of opening the kitchen door to get their wet food ready.

Your cats are already rubbing up against your leg before they are able to see or smell the food. The cat feels the same pleasure when opening the kitchen door, because it has been a reliable predictor for something nice to eat in the past. As a result, the sound and/or movement of the kitchen door triggers similar feelings.

These emotions take place both at the level of the species (primary emotions) and at the level of the individual (secondary emotions). While cats as a whole have certain expectations from their environment, an individual cat will also have certain expectations as a result of its own preferences. That which is valuable to the cat will trigger it.

Under-
standing
your cat's
behaviour

"Cats don't have complex thoughts, making their behaviour easy to interpret. Only when we try to interpret their behaviour in human terms will things go awry."
Anneleen Bru

INTERPRETING BEHAVIOUR

Our language contrasts sharply with the language of cats

Understanding our cats isn't always easy. We are inclined to interpret their behaviour from the perspective of our own forms of communication, human behaviour, habits and capacity for complex thought. This principle is called anthropomorphism, and must be avoided when observing cat behaviour, because it leads to misunderstandings and frustration.

Cats are unable to generate complex thoughts. As a result, they are unable to think in terms of the past of the future, and cannot imagine situations other than those occurring in the present moment. Cats live in the present.

Nevertheless, owners regularly interpret their cat's behaviour as jealous, naughty, lazy, angry or disappointed. However, we currently have no evidence that cats are able to have these types of complex, time-related feelings.

Distinguishing types of behaviour

'Behaviour' in itself is a vague term that covers many different meanings and covers all forms of behaviour a cat could possibly display. However, some of those forms of behaviour relate to the perception of certain triggers in the cat's environment, which the cat perceives using its senses. Other behaviours are subsequent responses to these perceptions.

A cat's response is determined by a long list of possible influences. Therefore, it's important to first create a subdivision of those influences.

1. Exposure to external stimuli

What triggers the cat? What is valuable to the cat? Consequently, what affects it, both at the level of the species and as an individual.

2. Perception through the senses

How does the cat perceive the world? What does it see, hear, smell and feel? Which body parts does it use for this?

3. Information processing

The external stimuli are run through the internal processing system which is influenced in turn by various factors including instincts, motivations, emotions, character traits and experiences

4. Response behaviour

The cat responds to the best of its ability and its behaviour clearly displays how it feels about things.

"Enabling your cat
to autonomously make
choices within its
territory is the key
towards a happy cat."
Anneleen Bru

YOUR CAT'S TERRITORY

Understanding territory

Your cat's territory consists of three large areas. In what follows, these three areas are graphically presented as neatly delineated areas, but in reality, your cat's territory actually consists of many small parts, places and passageways which together form the three parts.

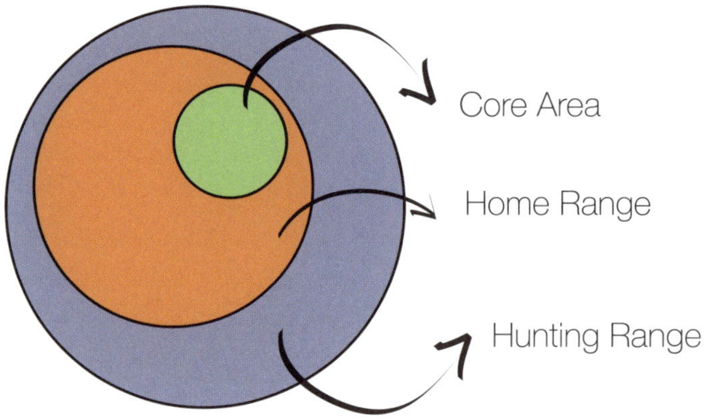

For a proper and clear overview, our starting point is the fact that every cat has a right to its own territory, consisting of three parts, that it doesn't have to share with others. Here, the cat can act according to its instincts and behave naturally, discharge energy and feel safe.

It is possible for cats to share part of their territory with other cats voluntarily, but this is very flexible, dependent on the environment, and preferably only with cats they can get along with very well.

So, a cat's territory consists of three parts: a small core area, a home range and a hunting area.

It is highly flexible and changes constantly (both in terms of its size and what the parts comprise), depending on the cat's choices and preferences; where is the cat safe, where does it find prey, where does it feel good and where can fun or tasty things be found?

Other influences are the sexual status of the cat (neutered or not), confidence level, previously learnt behaviour, the presence of other cats, relationships with other cats in the house, and so on.

What does the cat predominantly want to do here?

Core Area	Home Range	Hunting Area	
Core Area	Home Range	Hunting Area	
•			Sharing with group members
•			Eating safely
•			Drinking safely
•			Sleeping safely
	•		Drinking
	•		Using the litter tray
	•		Maintaining fixed walking routes
	•		Communicating through rubbing
		•	Communicating through scratching
		•	Communicating through spraying
•	•	•	Time sharing

FACT – Understanding territory in this way also clarifies quite a lot of behaviour.
What do you think of the following insights, for example?

> Cats like to eat their prey where its safe, in their core area. This is why they bring their prey home with them.
Naturally, they don't always want to eat their prey, because cats are given plenty of tasty biscuits and wet food to eat. Gifts? Not quite...

> Territories are highly flexible and prone to constant change.. Have you ever seen your cat sleeping in the same spot for months and then suddenly stop using that spot? That change means a shift in its core area and is perfectly normal!

A striking fact is that cats engage in 'time sharing' within their hunting range. They communicate with each other through smells to divide the area at certain times and use the area as efficiently as possible without meeting each other.

'You take this bit in the morning; in the evening, it's mine' and 'I own this bit by day and at night its yours' work well, especially among cats that are forced to make use of smaller areas, like in urban environments.

You have to rescale the previous representation of a cat's territory depending on where and how you live.

If you live in a large house, then the core area and possibly part of the home range will be within the house and the rest is outside of it.

However, if you live in an apartment and the cat isn't able to go outside, then all areas will be within the confinement of your home. In such cases, it is best to stimulate all phases and enrich all areas within your apartment. Not all at the same time of course, but in the appropriate and suitable places. The cat must, for example, be able to work for its food, hunt and play, scratch, climb, and so on.

EXERCISE - Draw a floor plan of your house and make two copies. On the first plan, map out all resources that are available to your cat.
On the second, indicate where your cat can often be found and which behaviour it displays (sleeping, eating, hunting) where.
Now, on the third plan, indicate all modifications you could implement to further separate and enrich your cat's three areas.
Subsequently, implement these adaptations step by step over a period of six weeks by placing extra resources and seeing if the cat's territory shifts.

"Cats are solitary
by necessity
but can also prefer
to be social."
Anneleen Bru

SOCIAL VS SOLITARY BEHAVIOUR

Social or solitary?

Let's get straight to the point: cats are neither social nor solitary. This is because cats adapt to their situation. Important factors are the behaviour of other cats, a cat's own experiences as a kitten and as an adult cat, its innate character (very social - antisocial) and the availability of resources in the environment.

The cat evolved as a solitary hunter over thousands of years, but if given a choice, it might not always prefer to live solitary. On the barren savannah, there isn't sufficient food for groups of cats. As a result, cats only hunt smaller prey.

As a result, cats don't need a social group with a fixed hierarchy in order to survive. The only time cats gather in the wild is during mating season and when mother cats have kittens. If there are too few resources, it's simply every cat for itself.

Does that mean cats prefer to be social and have many other cats around? No, absolutely not.
Cats still have their own individual characters, influenced by innate characteristics, the socialisation period (up to 16 weeks), during which kittens do or don't learn which social signals work in certain situations.

On top of that, there are (like with humans) mutual relationships. Sometimes there's chemistry between cats and sometimes there isn't. Their mutual relationship is also influenced by previous experiences they've had with other cats.

*Cats are not
solitary animals;
they are solitary hunters.*

Don't assume therefore that because your cat got along well with the previous cat, it will get along with all other cats. Because that unrealistic expectation is a foundation for tension in the house.

BEWARE!
Absolute necessities for cats to tolerate each other are, firstly, a proper, gradual introduction, and secondly, providing sufficient primary resources in the house, like eating locations and hiding places. Both in theory and in my practical experience, these two basic provisions keep returning as absolute musts for cats to adopt tolerant attitudes towards one another.

Even if your cats were born socially, were socialised well and have chemistry together, all this can be completely overturned if there are too few resources for the cats to do their own thing without getting in each other's way.

Social groups at home

Cats can form social groups at home. These groups are formed by cats that get along well, sleep together, play, groom each other and almost never hiss at each other.

These cats will share parts of their home range together, or at the very least, have a tolerant attitude towards its common use. The core area is sacred for all individual cats, and they prefer not to share it.

EXERCISE - Create an overview of the social groups at home by listing the names of your cats below:

Playing together ....

Grooming each other ....

Often rubbing up against each other ....

Seeking each other out throughout the day ....

Sleeping close to each other (<ten inches) ....

Staring at each other ....

Growling and/or hissing at each other ....

Walking away from another cat ....

Actively chasing another cat ....

Fighting with each other ....

TIP - We adopt the rule of sleeping at less than ten inches (25 cm) distance from each other, faced towards one another. It is not the case that two cats sleeping on one bed necessarily means they are part of the same social group. It could be the case that they were both motivated to lie there for a while and tolerate each other. Observe the distance between them and whether they are facing away from each other or towards one another.

Bowen and Heath have created a beautiful overview of social relationships or social groups among cats:

Pairs	A pair of cats, often from the same litter, that display friendly behaviour towards one another.
Cliques/Factions	Groups of three or more cats that display friendly behaviour towards one another but could possibly be aggressive towards other cats in the family.
Social Facilitators	These cats display and receive friendly signals from cats from multiple social groups (that do not get along), in this way spreading the common group scent between the cats.
Satellite Individuals	These cats barely receive nor display any friendly signals towards other cats in the family. They are more solitary and can sometimes find themselves in mildly aggressive situations with the other cats.
Despot Cats	These cats have no intention of living together with other cats and will intentionally chase other cats away and protect resources.

Source: Bowen, J., & Heath, S. (2005). Behaviour problems in small animals: practical advice for the veterinary team. Philadelphia, Pa: Elsevier Saunders. p. 198

Dominance among cats?

Dominance among cats does not exist.
Or more accurately, there is no decisive scientific evidence at present showing there is such a thing as dominance among cats. After all, why would a solitary hunter need a fixed, hierarchical group structure?

A fixed pecking order for an animal species that in itself is incredibly flexible in terms of its territory and social relationships, and merely depends on the available resources in the environment? That doesn't make sense, right?

As discussed previously, owners often confuse basic traits like confidence and motivation with dominance.

'Jasper is always first to the scene. He always eats first and the other cats are afraid of him. He is very dominant.' The description of the cat itself is correct in terms of its confident, prominent behaviour, but should not carry the label 'dominant'.

Jasper is a confident cat, with considerable motivation towards certain resources. Confident cats will more readily display a wider range of behaviour faster to get something, while shyer cats are more likely to be hesitant. You can therefore ask yourself: 'Why is it that one of my cats MUST act this way?' It's often territorial behaviour as a result of scarcity; there is too little present for all cats to get what they need individually. And of course this causes tension and fear.

Colonies of cats

In the wild, we can observe cats voluntarily forming colonies. There are usually groups of related female cats that primarily stick together to share the duties of caring for each other's kittens. They often display extensive friendly behaviour towards each other and nurse each other's kittens.

The big secret for the beautiful existence of these groups is also the presence of a sufficient number of resources; sufficient food, eating locations and hiding places.
If these conditions not been met, then the groups fall apart and each members goes his or her separate way.

Such a familial and matriarchal community formula differs strongly from how we keep our cats together. People often place unrelated male and female cats together. Our cats are neutered. Therefore, the mating season does not apply, and so on. As a result, it is especially important that we give sufficient attention to those necessary basic conditions and prevent scarcity from arising.

By providing plenty of resources in the environment, cats are placed in a position in which they CAN BE tolerant towards their own kind.

Sorry, not sorry

While cats can be sociable towards other cats, there is nonetheless a large sore point we should consider. As pointed out at the start of this book, cats are very limited in their repertoire of social signals, because throughout their evolutionary history, they never needed a group to survive.

They don't have any reconciliatory behaviour. This means: get out or fight! Cats can't say sorry, they cannot show they're sorry and they cannot make up after a conflict.

In principle, you should therefore never let cats 'fight it out'. This does not mean you should panic if your cats occasionally hiss or growl at each other. That's perfectly normal cat behaviour. It is good to be aware of the outcome. Does one cat leave or get out of the way when the other hisses? Mission accomplished. Because that's what the hissing cat is trying to achieve.

If the cat (or kitten) ignores the hissing or growling and simply continues doing what it's doing or doesn't leave or get out of the way, you as the owner or caregiver should intervene. Your cat might otherwise learn that her defensive behaviour doesn't work, leading to increased tension and emotions like fear and anxiety, causing or worsening problematic behaviour like aggression and spraying.

Introducing cats to one another

When cats see each other for the first time, they're really immediately enemies; that's their instinct. This is because they cannot run the risk of being injured by the other cat. Consequentially, cats need to be given time and space to 'learn' that the other cat doesn't pose a threat. And this 'learning' is not something they can do on their own.

Preparation

Firstly, make sure that your resources at home are doubled two weeks in advance. The cats will be redividing their home range, which they can only do if there are plenty of options and choices. Also, spread the resources well throughout your home.

Arrival

Set up your new cat in a separate space in which it has everything it needs. With that space as its home base, let it explore the rest of the house, without the presence of another cat. Ofcourse, allow the new cat to settle in first and get used to it's new environment. Observe its behaviour and make sure he's fine in this room before letting him go any further to the rest of the house.

Management

Before starting the introduction process, it is important that the cats aren't aware of another cat.
They shouldn't see each other through glass doors or windows, for example. They will probably hear and smell each other; there isn't much you can do to prevent this. But it is absolutely vital to wait with the introduction until the cats

are no longer displaying any stress responses to sounds and smells. This part alone could take several weeks.

The introduction

When both cats are happy, you can transition into the introduction process itself. Carefully follow the process step by step, because a good introduction is the best foundation for your cats to become friends.

Choose a door between two spaces, where both cats are familiar with their surroundings and can therefore eat calmly. Ideally, both cats are familiar with both spaces. This prevents one of the cats from suddenly becoming very interested in what's inside one of the spaces.

Find treats for both cats that they really love.
This could be wet food, fresh meat, cat treats or a drink, like cat milk. The aim in this is NOT to feed the cats as close to each other as possible. This will only have an opposite effect.

What you will be doing during an introduction is creating a positive association between the delicious food and the other cat.

This will cause your cat start thinking the other cat is a predictor for tasty food. This method enables you to effectively change a cat's experience of another cat as a threat.

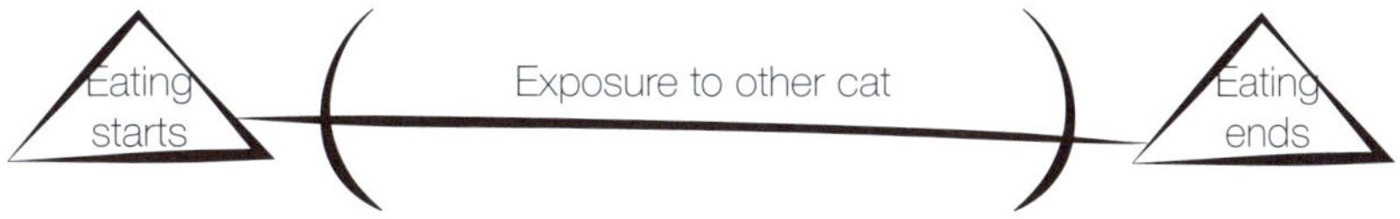

But you must take the time to go through the introduction process at a very slow pace, and respect the right timing.

Because timing is super important in the process!
Your cat's exposure to the other cat (seeing or hearing) must be 'sandwiched' between the opening and closing of the door.

This means that you can only leave the door ajar once both cats are on opposite sides of the closed door and calmly eating. Not before! And not for too long! Once the first cat is almost finished with its food, close the door again. There should be NO exposure without the extraction of tasty food.

Gradually build up their exposure with each training, leaving the door open wider, and taking a few steps back. For example, first leave the door open at half an inch, one inch, two inches, three inches, and so on.

Each time, both cats must be and remain calm. Therefore, pay close attention to subtle stress signals among both cats. If they're both okay, you can open the door a few inches wider during the next session.

Also, play around with the locations of both cats. Sometimes, seeing each other from a distance; so far that they really don't realise the other cat is there. But, at other times, have one sitting behind the door and another in view.

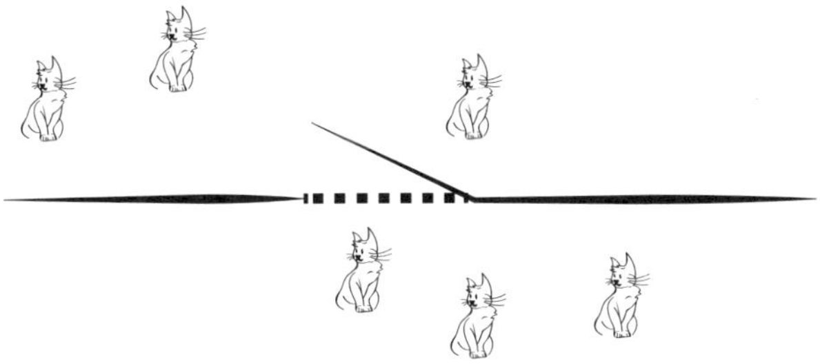

Do this training one to two times a day. Each training should last only a few minutes. The rest of the time the cats must live entirely separate from each other again, as though they do not exist to one another.

The only way that two cats can develop good, positive associations with each other, is by making their exposure to one another wholly take place during training sessions and only in the presence of tasty food they're both enjoying. If the cats also meet outside of the training moments, there is the chance that they will create instinctive and possibly negative associations with each other during uncontrolled situations. In such cases, the training moments will barely generate any results. Make sure to prevent the cats from seeing each other through glass doors, and so on.

If one of the cats is not very motivated by the food, you can use other 'primary' distractors. In other words, things that motivate and distract the cat, like valerian pouches, catnip toys or moving toys. Sadly, stroking usually isn't enough to truly motivate your cat.

Once you have been using the training process for two to three weeks and you are able to open the door entirely, you can start building up the duration. This means that you will be leaving the door open after the cats have eaten for gradually longer periods. The same applies to fun distractions, like treats, valerian or other herbal toys, playing with the rod, and so on.

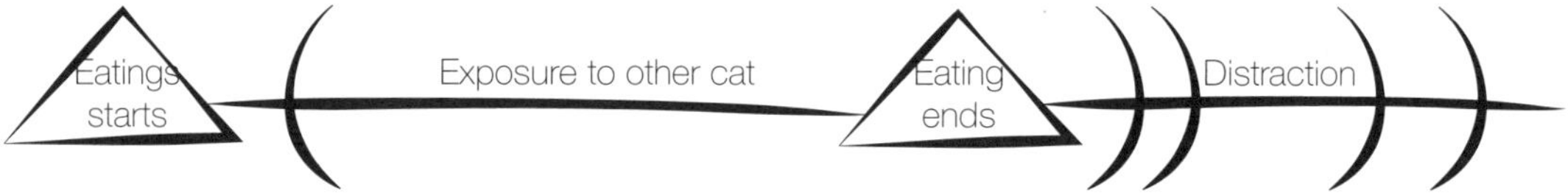

You should also build this up gradually. When things are going well, keep adding a few seconds without the fun distraction, but be alert. This will teach the cats what it's like to simply be around each other without something fun happening.

The moment will arrive when the cats want to start sniffing each other. It's perfectly normal if they hiss at one another.

Leave them be for a few seconds, but then immediately introduce a fun distraction.

Continue repeating this, until you notice them seeking each other out and largely feeling comfortable with this.

Here, you will also be gradually building up the time after uneventful training sessions. First half a minute, then a minute, then several minutes, then ten minutes, fifteen minutes, until you can leave the door open.

After that, only separate the cats when you're not at home, until you're entirely sure they like each other.

The above way of introducing them to each other may not appear to be the simplest process, but it is the ideal way to minimise the chance of a negative relationship developing between cats.

Sadly, it's not an exact science, but get started with it, play around with it a little, and during the process, remain attentive of subtle stress signals among both cats.

Understanding your cat's language

With communication as part of the cat's ethology, it's all about the effective message, in the shape of signals that cats broadcast to themselves, to other cats and to us.

In practice, we see that the misinterpretation of the signals their cats are sending often causes frustration and confusion among owners. Because owners often interpret their cat's behaviour from the perspective of their own, human patterns of communication.

This is why in this chapter we want to shine a light on the most important signals cats send out and what these signals look like. The signals send a message to the cat's surroundings, while at the same time they communicate something about how the cat feels.

By learning to look at typical cat signals, learning to better understand and 'read' them, we are able to respond to them correctly. We can, for example, adapt the environment or our own behaviour, and are given the option of approaching the cat in ways it understands, thereby improving our mutual relationship.

Influencing your cat with your own behaviour

Our response to the cat's behaviour can influence its general well-being. Well, as long as you know which signals to look for to truly understand its behaviour.

Here are a few simple rules, which aren't always easy to follow according to owners, but could have a positive effect on your cat.

- If your cat is feeling stressed already, at least you won't make things worse.
- We do not reward undesirable behaviour.
- Your cat feels safer when it's left alone.
  This means your cat prefers not to be comforted when it isn't feeling good. Cats are and will remain solitary hunters that want to be alone when they're not feeling their best.

What can you do with the info in the upcoming chapter? You will understand your cat's language, read its mood and respond to it in the right way!

A few golden rules to positively influence your cat's behaviour when observing certain things:

Ignore all forms of unhappy behaviour and stress signals (not only the clear signals, but also the subtler ones). Additionally, find out what you can change in the environment to prevent your cat from feeling this way. Change whatever you can change.

Reward happy (only if you're entirely sure) behaviour with something THE CAT likes, like giving it treats or playing with it. Stroking is not something cats inherently enjoy (sensitive fur), which doesn't usually make it a good way to validate good behaviour.

Is your cat easily fearful by character? Evoke positive behaviour by throwing a treat or make a toy appear out of nowhere. Make sure the cat isn't aware that you're doing anything, but is focused on the treat, toy or the rod instead. Once she shows happier behaviour, you can give her some lovely attention. You will see your cat behave more confidently within a few weeks by applying this technique. The cat will slowly start to feel safer, and therefore also feel happier.

"A cat's whiskers and tail
can tell you how the cat is
feeling in a split second."
Anneleen Bru

VISUAL COMMUNICATION

Reading cat language

Visual communication is about reading the cat's body language. You can look at a small part of the cat, like its tail, ears or whiskers, but you also need to look at the cat's entire body and what it's doing.

In some cases, we can read how the cat is feeling by looking at parts of its body. Although we should not lose sight of the rest of the body, and the body as a whole. Sometimes the signals a cat's body sends out can be contradictory. In such cases, it is advisable to be on the safe side. Leave your cat alone for a little while. It might be feeling stressed.

We should also be watchful not to confuse 'observant' behaviour with 'response' behaviour, as further discussed in the chapter on ethology.

When I ask the following question in my training sessions: 'Which body part can immediately show you how the cat is feeling?', people often respond in unison: 'The ears!' If I then ask: 'Ah, and what do the ears tell you?' 'Which feeling can be read from which position of the ears?' - long silence. Exactly, you can't infer a lot from them, unless the message is very clear.

Has a cat flattened its ears while it is growling and hissing? It's clear how it feels. There's no need to come to one of our training programmes to find this out.
But ears that rotate and are directed forward - that's purely observant behaviour. The cat is listening and hasn't

responded to what it's hearing yet. There is no response behaviour yet. Thus, there's no way to know how the cat is feeling yet.

In principle, the cat could do all kinds of things; walk away, explore, hide, and so on. What you are able to see is that the cat is on guard, because it's listening and observing. But that doesn't communicate any information about how its feeling.

Reading stress with cats

When you start to read your cat's body language based on what we're discussing here, and would like to determine whether or not your cat is stressed, it is important to differentiate between positive and negative stress.

In the world of behaviour, stress is a form of tension in response to external stimuli in order to survive. In that sense, it can be both positive and negative. And the fact that stress has a considerable impact on behaviour and feelings is something we as people also occasionally experience.

Think of what stress does to your body: you lose your appetite (or eat more), your heart beats faster, you breathe faster and your body gets ready to make a move (fight, flight or freeze). This is because your 'sympathetic nervous system' shoots into action when you feel threatened, like during a conflict, quarrel, fight or loss.

However, that same sympathetic nervous system starts up when something exciting happens which you do not immediately experience as a threat, but which demands action. Think of being in love, taking an exam, applying for a job, playing a competitive game, and so on.

Thus, stress isn't necessarily a bad thing, but required to live and survive. Therefore, don't sound the alarm if you observe stress signals from your cat, but look at the circumstances: what is the cat doing, what has it just done and what was it about to do?

If you still think the cat is experiencing unpleasant stress, there is nothing you can do except ignore it while at the same time making sure the situation is not repeated in the future.

To do this, ask yourself what you can do to avoid those things that cause the cat stress and which other tools you can give it to deal with stress (more effectively).

By now, we know that the largest stress factor for animals isn't the trigger itself, but rather, the manner in which it is able to deal with it. Does the cat have choices available in its response to the situation? If so, it will experience less stress than in situations in which it doesn't have any options to choose from.

Tails

Happy tails

A cat walking around with its tail up is completely fine. The cat has seen something it likes; it's exploring.

When a cat has its tail pointing upwards in the shape of a question mark, it wants to greet you and is happy to see you.

When a cat is very excited, she will keep her tail pointing straight upwards, also known as 'dry spraying'. Luckily, no urine is released!

A tail trailing behind the cat's body in a relatively horizontal position is a neutral signal.

Unhappy tails

One of the most often missed stress signals among cats is a low-hanging tail close to the ground. These cats don't want to be seen, because they feel threatened. Therefore, make absolutely sure not to give them attention and leave them alone when you spot this behaviour and this tail.

Cats whose tails are wagging (both the tip and the whole tail) are showing you they are annoyed. This irritation should be seen within the framework of what is currently happening. If you're stroking your cat, it's best to stop. If your cat has spotted prey, let it be. It's excited!

When a cat makes its tail bigger, it feels threatened and wants to keep the something approaching at bay by making itself bigger.

Whiskers

Most cat owners have never paid attention to their cat's whiskers, while this is one of the easiest and fastest way to find out how your cat is feeling. When the whiskers are pressed against the cat's cheeks, it doesn't feel good and wants to protect its whiskers.

If your cat is walking around or sleeping with its whiskers pressed close to its cheeks, it isn't entirely happy, and best left alone. Of course, this isn't the case all the time.

At other times, the cat will retracts its whiskers, because they would otherwise get in the way. It does this while sniffing, eating and drinking, for example. Therefore, pay close attention to the present situation and why your cat might have her whiskers pressed to its cheeks.

Cats that have their whiskers pointing entirely forward are happy and often excited. The cat is either happy or has just spotted prey. However, in extreme situations, the whiskers will also be pointing forward. If they're standing eye to eye with another cat, for example. Naturally, this situation clearly points towards a cat that isn't happy.

A neutral position among cats is when the whiskers are pointing straight outwards, perpendicular to the cat's nose.

Eyes

An often heard statement is that a cat's eyes can tell us how it is feeling. In extreme situations, like with very frightened cats, this could be the case.

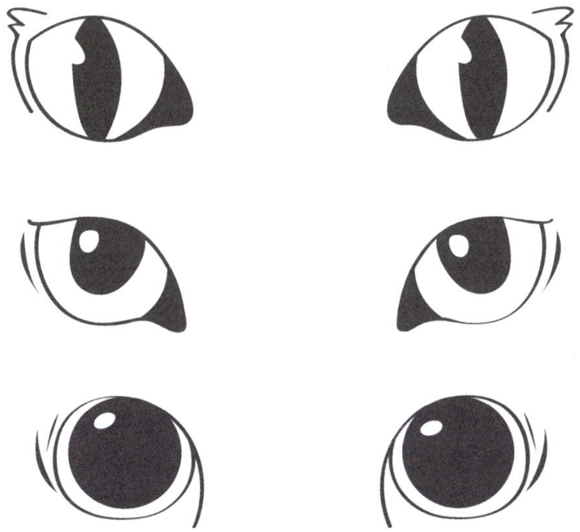

When the pupils are so large that the eyes are almost completely black, it is true that the cat is very scared, and you must take immediate action to increase its sense of safety.

The pupils of a cat that has spotted something can take on different shapes; from very small and narrow to oval. It is hard to infer anything from this.

Moreover, the size of a cat's pupils has as much to do with light entering the eye as with underlying emotions.

Something that does tell us more about the cat's behaviour and how it feels is the position of the eyelids. A cat whose eyes are wide open is staring, which often means there's something threatening around. It either wants to chase away something coming towards it or has just spotted prey.

Staring is something extremely aggressive for cats. Many threatening indoor and outdoor staring contests go unnoticed by us, because they take place very subtly. They can occur at a few inches or several yards from one another. But in any case, things ARE NOT fine! This is because the cats are locked in a face off which they cannot easily get out of themselves. Because if one of the two decides to leave, the other cat will simply go straight after the cat attempting to leave. Not great for your survival chances in nature.

TIP - Be aware of staring moments between cats. Grab hold of a visual barrier, like a newspaper or a pillow, and, very calmly and without talking, place it between the cats. Softly push the more confident cat away, so that the more troubled cat has the opportunity to leave. If they seek each other out again to stare or growl, separate them from each other for a few hours, so that their stress levels can subside.

I meet people who tell me they always attract cats, while they have absolutely no affinity towards them or simply don't even like cats. Why is that?

Imagine you're a cat and on the African savannah, and you spot a creature ten times your size walking towards you while staring. To make matters worse, the strange, large creature also wants to touch you, and lift you off the ground entirely!

What, in such cases, have thousands of years of evolution taught you? To scurry, of course! However, what about when a large creature doesn't pay you any attention, shows its rear to you and respectfully avoids eye contact? Now that's friendly!

What would you as a cat do? Who would you approach?

TIP - Do you want to show your cat real affection, like a cat? Then, slowly close your eyes while looking at it. Ordinarily, your cat will respond by doing the same, provided it feels comfortable. If your cat isn't relaxed, this can also be a method to make it feel more at ease, although there's no guarantee. If your cat slowly closes its eyes, make sure to do the same. This builds trust.

Tongue

It's a subtle stress signal when a cat briefly licks its upper lip when it hasn't just been eating or drinking. If so, it has just smelt or experienced something that isn't to its liking. The cat responds to this by licking.

Mouth

Cats use their mouths while yawning as a way to discharge stress, unless they've just woken up. When things happen that the cat needs to process, it yawns as a way to deal with this.

On top of that, yawning is the perfect way to let your cat know everything is okay. It has a stress discharging - and therefore relaxing - effect. Incidentally, yawning also works with dogs. It might look a bit funny, but it works a treat!

TIP - If your cat is having a hard time, yawn a few times in succession and softly close your eyes, without approaching it. Your cat will most likely also respond with a yawn and a dropping of the eyelids. Be aware that this 'trick' only works in cases of subtle stress. Don't try this if the cat is very stressed.

Paws

A cat's paws are its sixth sense. They are exceptionally sensitive because the little hairs between the paw pads are so close together. We know that cats have blurry vision at distances under one metre, which makes their front paws particularly important tools to locate prey and investigate things, especially in the dark.

FACT - Research has shown that female cats prefer to use their right paw and male cats prefer their left paw. This behaviour is consistently shown by cats older than one year old.

Cats also use their paws for kneading. It is the leftover behaviour from when they were kittens and would knead their mother's belly to stimulate the production of milk while suckling. This is the initial situation in which this behaviour is shown, but it also has an important comforting function at a later age. This is due to the remaining association of safety and happiness while suckling close to their mummy.

Cats do it when they feel good, but also if they aren't feeling good and are trying to comfort themselves. Kneading is more common among kittens that were separated from their mothers too soon (before they were twelve weeks old), because of that comforting function.

This kneading behaviour is perfectly normal and only becomes problematic if the cat starts effectively biting holes in fabrics or other things, and starts eating inedible things. This phenomenon is called 'pica' and is a behavioural problem that demands a thorough and expert analysis.

TIP - Because of the sensitivity of cats' paws, it is best not to touch them too much. If you need to get to the paws for grooming or to check them - when cutting the nails or tending to a wound, for example - give the cat ample time to learn that touching its front paws is okay. Do this by training the cat.

First, find a delicious treat the cat loves. Then, start by placing your finger near its paw (not touching it yet) and giving the cat a treat. Next, softly and quickly touch the paw again, giving the cat another treat. Gradually go one step further, combined with taking a step back each time. Make sure that the cat is not or does not become stressed, and that it is so focused on the treat that it hardly notices you doing something with its paw. In this way, as with previous exercises, you can create a positive association between the touching of the paw and the tasty treat that follows. This allows you to influence the cat's experience again.

Fur

We previously read about the cat's fur being exceptionally sensitive. What can we infer from a cat's fur?

When you observe small twitches towards the back of your cat's back, this indicates that the cat is irritated. This could be caused by both a physical irritation (such as a flea bite or an allergy) or a behavioural irritation. The cat might be irritated by its fur being touched or an external trigger exciting it (like prey or a threat). Do you observe small twitches towards the back of the cat's fur? Make sure to stop whatever you are doing and give the cat a chance to walk away.

The manner in which a cat looks after its fur can have different meanings. A cat grooming itself effectively is sitting quietly, feels comfortable and makes long licks of its fur with its tongue.

However, does the cat stop abruptly while walking to quickly lick its front paw or lower back? If so, the cat is temporarily stressed and confused. The cat's deciding what to do next; 'will I go left, right, up, down, walk away or attack?', and so on. This type of behaviour is sometimes also referred to as 'displacement behaviour' and is the fourth 'F' within the theory of stress responses. We already mentioned 'fight, flight and freeze' and can now add 'fiddle', which derives from the expression 'to fiddle about'.

"What a wonderful world would open to us if only we could smell what our cats smell."
Anneleen Bru

COMMUNICATION THROUGH SMELLS

Communicating with their noses

Cats communicate with their noses. It is the most efficient way to get results as a solitary hunter. The cat has an extra organ in its palate that enables it to absorb social smells through its saliva. This is called a 'flehmen' response.

Cats primarily communicate by secreting pheromones (or rather, their more complex form, called semiochemicals) in their environment and on other cats, depending on what they want to achieve. By leaving smells in the environment (and on other cats), the cat can communicate with itself and other cats through both time and space.

The two most important reasons for an animal to communicate is to keep itself safe and to either attract other cats or to get out of their way. For a cat, it is at least as important to communicate with itself ('is it safe or not?') as it is to communicate with other cats ('do we want to see each other or do we prefer not to?').

We as humans cannot smell their pheromones, since we don't belong to the same species as cats.

This is because pheromones serve as a mode of communication between animals of the same species. What we can perceive are the visual signals that are part of secreting pheromones.

Thus, they also allow us to learn about where the cat feels what way. This is because the communication signals used tell us a tremendous amount about the cat's emotional state.

Cats secrete smells in three different ways; by nuzzling, scratching and spraying.

The function of the cat's rubbing, scratching or spraying will be mostly determined by the territory it is in (core area, home range or hunting area). The cat's behaviour is a response to how it feels in a particular location.

Cats observe things in one of the three living areas with all their senses. They process these signals based on previous experiences, instincts, motivations and emotions, and, depending on the feeling they experience, display particular behaviour; running away, investigating further, adopting a defensive posture, and so on.

When the cat passes through the same area again next time, the secreted scent trail will tell it how to behave and how it felt last time. Should the cat be on its guard, for example? Or can it let its guard down?

At home, you can probably see yellowish spots appearing at withers height in the corners of rooms or on door frames.

These spots are most likely along your cat's fixed walking route, where it secretes its facial pheromones multiple times a day.

It is important for your cat that you do not clean these spots. You will merely be cleaning important communication signals.

On the other hand, it is best to properly clean up spraying spots. This will prevent the cat from wanting to spray there again. Of course, we should combine this with adaptations in the house to reduce stress.

TIP - What is the best way to clean up urine or spraying spots?
Take three empty water sprayers and fill them with:

1. Ten parts water and one part enzymatic, organic detergent
2. Water
3. Alcoholic solution (at least 70%)

A. First, clean up the urine with a small cloth.
B. Then, clean the spot with each water sprayer.
C. Allow it to dry properly in between.

VOCAL COMMUNICATION

Meowing

However much we'd like it to be the case, vocal communication isn't as important to cats as it is to us.

As solitary hunters, there is no point bellowing 'meeeeoooowww' across the desert. Nobody will hear you, so it's a wasted effort. There is no point whatsoever meowing if the closest other cat is a few miles away. That's why cats use smells as their primary language. In addition, loud, vocal communication can lead to unsafe situations and attract enemies or larger predators to your hiding places.

Cats do, however, learn that making sounds attracts our attention. As pack animals, we humans are programmed to be alert and triggered by anything that sounds like the sound of a baby. Meowing is like weeping to us. This is also the reason that the sirens of emergency services sound the way they do; it is a universally stimulating sound that everybody who hears it responds with alertness.

Cats meowing falls into the same category. We are triggered and instinctively look in the direction of the sound, usually followed by a response of giving attention, treats, providing outdoor access, and so on. From a young age, our cats learn: 'Oh, this works! If I want something from my human, I will meow.'

Cats can learn this very situationally; simply by trying it at certain times during the day, they know exactly from which person and in which room they can get what they need or want. Additionally, they know at what tone and with how many decibels to meow. Cats have trained us well - the opportunistic little rascals!

Use of vocal sounds

Cats primarily use sounds, both vocally and non-vocally, in conflict situations and during mating season. However, there is also communication of this kind between a mother and her offspring. Because we live close to our cats, they also use vocal and non-vocal sounds towards people. Most households have several subtle moments of tension. Obvious tension is often dealt with quickly with therapy or resettlement. On top of this, our domestic cats are neutered and the average family doesn't have an annual litter of kittens.

Types of sounds

In scientific literature, sounds are divided into three categories:

1. Sounds that are produced with a closed mouth, like purring and cute 'prrrrtt' sounds cats make as greetings.
2. Sounds that involve the mouth opening and closing, like meowing, crying or chattering.
3. And finally, sounds that are produced with an open mouth, like puffing (quickly expressing air), spitting, hissing, growling and yowling during a conflict.

Purring

We've all heard of purring. Cats do it when they feel comfortable, when they're enjoying something, or as a form of greeting. It is a way for them to communicate that they don't feel threatened.

Cats also purr when they feel very ill or when they feel threatened. It's their way of saying that they aren't a threat themselves, in the hope of being allowed to escape. There are also cats that never purr, and that is perfectly fine.

TIP - We always advise being aware of sudden changes in your cat's behaviour. Has your cat always purred, but has it suddenly stopped? Or did it never purr before and is purring now? These are times when it's best to contact a vet.

If you are dealing with feral cats, it's important to be aware of this. In practice, I often see volunteers who interpret a feral cat's purring behaviour as a signal that it is starting to feel better.

Nothing could be further from the truth. The cat purrs to comfort itself and make it clear that it doesn't want to be a threat. This means its stress level is very high, making it impossible for the cat to learn anything new. This includes learning that people aren't a threat. In the way, also be wary of a rigid posture, the cat's whiskers and potentially dilated pupils. The cat might also stop eating, because stress suppresses the sensation of hunger. It could become very sick if the stress continues for too long.

Chattering

Chattering is the adorable behaviour cats display when they see a fly on the wall or a bird outside. It's like babbling. They display this behaviour when they feel the frustration of not being able to (immediately) reach their prey. A recent study concluded that it might be a call to attract prey towards them.

"Stress among cats starts with
closed eyes, a tongue flick, a
small twitch in the fur, whiskers
facing backward. Let's please
give this our attention. Your cat
is trying to tell you something."
Anneleen Bru

SUMMARY: READING CAT BEHAVIOUR

Cat is at ease/happy

- Whiskers facing forward
- Ears facing forward
- Small pupils
- Tail pointing upward in the shape of a question mark sign
- Dry spraying as a greeting
- Playing
- Sleeping on its back
- Closing its eyes
- Purring

Expectant attitude

- Standing straight, tail draped over its paws
- Sleeping while hunched
- Hiding (visual barrier)
- Rolling around the ground
- Yawning (not if it has just woken up)
- Stretching (not if it has just woken up)
- Whiskers pointing outward (neutral)

Subtle stress signals

- Tail close to the ground
- Whiskers facing backward
- Licking (the mouth)
- Twitches in the fur (at the back)
- Wagging of the tail (tip/entire tail)
- Short licks of the fur/base of the tail
- Lifting a paw
- Ears pointed outward
- Staring
- Scratching (excitement, + or -)
- Pretending like it's asleep

Clear stress signals

- Growling
- Hissing
- Spitting
- Crying
- Yowling
- Ears flat
- Large round pupils
- Fur standing on end (tail, back)
- Purring (very ill, last resort)

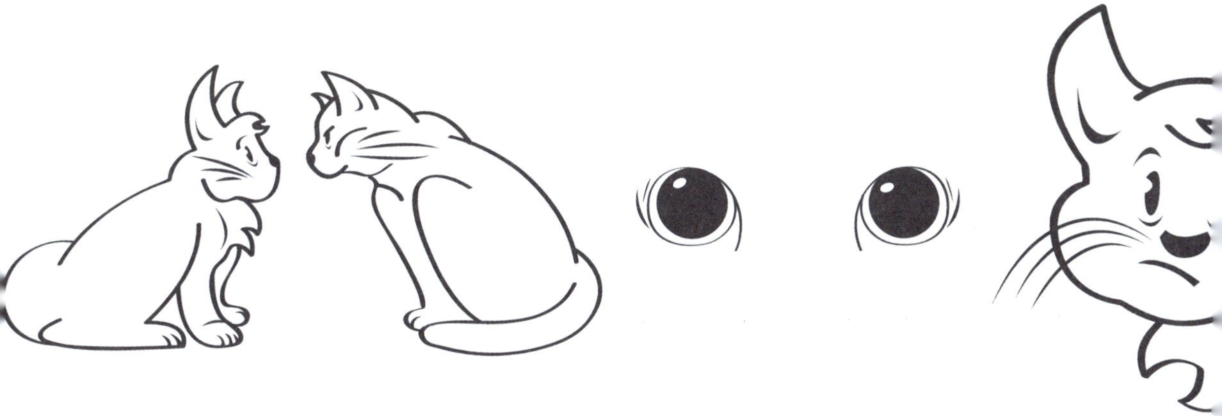

Optimising the environment

Understanding cat needs

We often view cats from the perspective of our own behaviour. We expect certain things from them, because they are important to us. Most of the misconceptions I see in practice are about providing vital resources and showing each other affection.

In areas where we should be treating cats more like people we don't do so enough. An example is providing plenty of eating locations and hygienic conditions.

As social animals, we each have our own plate and our own chair at the table. Nonetheless, cats, as solitary hunters, are obliged to share their eating locations with other cats in the household. For them, it's about locations, not the number of bowls.

Another example is the litter tray. Do you like doing your business in a filthy toilet? Don't we also make sure the toilet is in proper condition for its next use? Still, we often come across cats with house soiling problems because the owner only empties the litter tray every few days.

This is actually abusing cats' incredible instinct for cleanliness. So, of course there are occasionally cats that say: 'No, thank you. This toilet is too dirty for me. I won't do my business here.' Understandable, isn't it?

At other times, we treat our cats too much like humans when we should be taking their typical primary cat traits into consideration.

Think, for example, of walking towards at your cat, making strong eye contact. This behaviour comes across as very threatening to cats. When on the North African savannah and a large creature comes walking up to you while staring at you, you'd be advised to run!

It's important to list all of your cat's primary needs. In this way, a few small adaptations in your home can make a tremendous difference in the well-being and daily routine of your cats.

Don't be deterred - the following chapter is primarily intended to inspire and give you extra insights by providing tips.

So, if at any point you think: 'My cat doesn't have a problem with that, so I'm not going to change that.' I am still going to ask you to implement the change and try it out. Your cat might not have had a problem with something, because until now, it never had any other options. Who knows, your cat might become even happier! You will be surprised!

The common threads in a cat's existence are predictability, recognisability and safety.

As mentioned previously, a cat is continuously busy scanning and sizing up its environment.
The three most important properties of a good environment are: predictability, recognisability and safety. As a good cat owner, it is best to memorise these three words.

Cats are incredibly sensitive to stress by virtue of their incredible evolutionary adaptability, which has enabled them to survive as solitary hunters for thousands of years. But, in our households, that same sensitivity to stress means cats are aware of everything.

Predictability

Predictability in the environment means a cat can create a predictable routine for itself. That routine is important to anticipate potential scenarios concerning threatening or dangerous situations.

Doors that are closed sometimes and open at other times are not predictable. Litter trays in other places at night than during the day are equally unpredictable. Owners who sometimes stroke the cat briefly and sweetly and at other times are pulling tangles from its hair are equally unpredictable.
Owners who sometimes respond to the cat's signals and sometimes ignore them are equally unpredictable.
Do you have a cat at home that meows by a closed door, but doesn't want to come through when you open the door? The cat's not concerned with getting through the

door, but rather, the fact that the door must be open in case it needs to get through to respond to imminent danger. A cat wants to have choices, remember? So keep all options open.

If you place a cardboard box in your house, at first, your cat will use the box a lot. It's new and fun, and it's an ideal hiding place. After a while, the cat will start to use the box less or will no longer use it at all. You decide to remove the box, because you think your cat's fed up with it, doesn't like it any more or doesn't need it any longer. False! This is where things go wrong. The box is a predictable hiding place for the cat that it can use any time there is the threat of danger, but which it doesn't have to use.
The presence of the box ensures your cat feels comfortable and can walk around calmly. If you dispose of the box (because it seems something temporary), your cat will think: 'Darn, now I have to be on my guard again, because my trusted, predictable, in-case-of-emergency hiding place is gone!'

Your cat needs choices throughout its territory. This means it must be given multiple options per item or source it would like to use. Having choices doesn't mean something is simply present, but that there are multiple versions or options of things for it to choose from. 'Will I go here? Or eat there? Shall I use the litter tray on the second floor or on the ground floor?' Your cat makes its decisions based on safety, personal preferences, and previously learnt behaviour. This way of making decisions creates peace and predictability, because the cat learns that it will always be able to choose a safe option 'if' it needs something.

Familiarity

Familiarity is about whether your cat is given the chance to label things, so that it knows what to do next time it passes through. We already delved deeper into this in the chapter about pheromones and communication through smells. Must the cat be on guard? Can it be at ease? Or should it flee? The cat will secrete scent trails at specific, distinctive and important places throughout its territory. These smell properties and its previous experiences will determine whether the cat recognises its environment and feels at ease or not.

Therefore, if you introduce a new cat into your home, buy a new sofa or renovate part of your house, give your cat plenty of alone time to sniff everything and explore. Provide plenty of source options (more than one, at the very least!), so the cat can discover and label its new environment at its own pace. Does this mean you cannot change anything in your home? Of course not! Needless to say, we must remain realistic. Your cat will be more capable of dealing with things as long as you give it the time and tools to discover everything and apply its scent trails. This contributes to your cat's well-being and happiness. And that's exactly what this book is about!

Safety

It's a given that it is best for the environment in which your cat spends its time to be free from stress factors or imminent threats (like strange cats, loud sounds and large, unknown dogs).

However, safety also encompasses the indirect form, such as accessible and efficient passageways within its territory, the accessibility of primary resources and also the means and support elements to deal with danger. It isn't only about what we offer our cat, but also the manner in which (how), the place and location (where), and the options and times at which (when) we offer these things.

Here are a few examples to outline this:

EXAMPLE - Rebecca provides food and drink for her cats in the kitchen and has the litter tray in the adjoining utility room. There is one door from the living room to the kitchen. This creates stress because both Ines and her boyfriend often use this doorway as a passageway, but also because if another cat were to sit in the doorway, the cat's passageway to ALL resources would be blocked. And cats are known to block access to primary resources if they're located in the same place. Because cats have a scarcity mindset, confident cats will not think twice about guarding resources and keeping them all to themselves. Solitary hunters, remember? Because the passageway is unpredictable and unsafe, her cats experience stress whenever they want to eat, drink and use the litter tray. On top of that, they spend their whole days feeling anxious in anticipation of these moments ('when I want to eat something later, there is a chance that ...').

EXAMPLE - A current living trend is to place beautiful, patio doors that reach down to the floor. This is one of the biggest stress factors for cats, because they can constantly be threatened by unknown cats outside staring in. Staring between cats is extremely aggressive (even though it may appear like they're having a 'friendly' look at one another) and, as a result, your cat will be on its guard and unable to peacefully make use of all the resources you have provided for it in this space. Therefore, stick opaque film from the bottom of the window to just above the height of a standing cat. Ignorance is bliss.

AVOIDING SCARCITY

Scarcity vs abundance

Scarcity of resources does not necessarily mean there aren't enough items or resources, but it does mean there are insufficient choices. A cat wants to and therefore must be able to choose at which location it prefers to use an item or source. On top of that, cats must be able to make this choice in a predictable way. Providing choices creates a sense of control and safety. This allows your cat to make the correct, safe and appropriate choice at any given time.

This means your cat should never only have one option in terms of any primary source, and it is always best to provide an extra backup option if there is more than one cat in the household. Therefore, the rule is n+1 number of locations. This means counting the number of cats, and adding one backup. Thus, it's not about how many items or resources are provided at one location, because this still counts as one from the cat's perspective. If you place five bowls in the same place, for example, this is still just one source.

Adopting the n+1 rule means your cat can make choices throughout the day: 'Ah, it's no longer safe there, because my sister is eating there and we don't like to eat together, so I'll go into the bedroom to eat' or 'I have to pee, but Balou is on the lookout in the hallway upstairs. I don't like that, so I'll choose to use the litter tray in the bedroom'. Cats are opportunists and must always be given an opportunity to make their own choices. Understandable, isn't it? Aren't we the same?

Cats like to do everything alone; eating, drinking, sleeping, hunting, hiding, scratching, and so on. So make sure that, for each of these functions, there are plenty of options for each cat, and that they are spread out and accessible in a variety of ways. Many of my clients have special 'cat rooms', in which all resources are gathered in a single room. This isn't ideal for a group of cats.

A cat wants to have everything spread out throughout the house. This is the only way it can make choices. This is the reason I personally am not a fan of traditional cat trees, because they unite too many functions; height, hiding places and scratching. A cat needs to have these three different functions spread out throughout its territory in the three different areas (core area, home range, hunting area) - not all just in the same place. On top of that, these scratching posts aren't exactly visually appealing. As a result, people often prefer to hide them away in the corner of the house so that they aren't bothered by them. And, while owners may believe they have met all of the cat's needs, this is precisely where cats don't need those functions.

N+1 is the golden rule from which you must not deviate.

Furnishing the environment

Supermarket phase

We want to optimise the cat's environment so that it feels happy in it. But how do we know what to position where, and what your cat likes and doesn't like? There's only one possible answer: experiment! This is why I always talk of a 'supermarket phase'; a period of four to six weeks in which we give the cat multiple options and let it choose. This means gritting your teeth for six weeks, and letting your partner or housemates know that the excessive number of resources on offer won't be forever.

To start this period, don't remove any familiar or predictable items, or change their position; only add a few things. As a rule for the number of locations during the supermarket phase, use (n+1) x 2 (with fewer than five cats) or nx2 (with five or more cats).

During this period, your cats have the opportunity to redivide their territories, and to learn from experience what are safe choices for them. Afterwards, you can gradually take away those items which were never used.

For families with cats that are having difficulties or larger groups in which there is tension, you can repeat the supermarket phase every year. Things might have changed in the environment, at your neighbour's house and in the individual preferences of the cats at home. Also, repeat the supermarket phase with the death of a cat or the arrival of a new cat. It's during these times that there is a high need to redivide the resources and the available area.

IKEA, etc.

Regular clients in my practice sometimes jokingly ask me if I own shares in IKEA, because I send them to 'ordinary' people shops - like IKEA, TK Maxx or charity shops - for cat things.

Items that are enriching for cats don't always have to be expensive, from speciality shops or pet shops. Be creative, explore, create your own and experiment!

In other words, go to places where you can find what your cat needs and not the other way round.

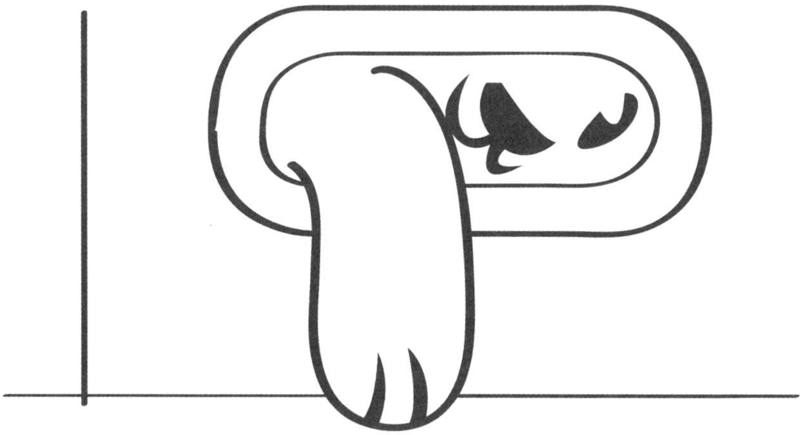

"By placing resources in the right places, we create a predictable and recognisable environment. Cats will be so happy for this."
Anneleen Bru

SAFE OR UNSAFE?

The two types of areas for a happy cat's household

To gain a clear overview of what a cat truly needs in the house to be happy, in practice, we divide the cats necessary resources over two types of areas; the 'SAFE' area and the 'UNSAFE' area.

SAFE concerns primary resources which must be provided in safe places, to ensure they are safely accessible to the cat at all times and in a predictable way. Safe places are hidden corners, under desks, between the cupboard and the wall, and so on; places where there isn't much happening or passing by and where the cat won't be frightened by sudden sounds, smells or movements. If your cat's resources aren't freely accessible, your cat will develop generalised anxiety, which doesn't only affect its behaviour and general well-being, but also has a damaging impact on its health. Chronic stress can result in illness, urinary tract and bladder problems. A body in stress is not receptive to food, for example. As a result, the cat will vomit more easily, or may stop eating entirely.

UNSAFE refers to the tools or support your cat needs to deal with threats or resources of danger. Because an imminent threat alone isn't a problem, *if* you see it coming and can therefore decide how to deal with it.

By providing certain items in unsafe places, you give your cat the tools it needs to estimate potential threats in a predictable way, and deal with threats effectively at the places they occur.

As a result, your cat will have a generally calmer attitude, since you've made its environment predictable and controllable.

Examples of unsafe places are passageways, doorways, landings, stairwells, hallways, spaces by the front or back door, areas near waste bins in the garage, cat flaps, and all other places where there is a considerable chance your cat might run into other cats or where there could be commotion, like in the kitchen or the lounge.

SAFE	UNSAFE
Food	Scratching places
Water	Heights
Litter trays	Visual barriers
+ scratching places + heights + visual barriers	+ water

You are certainly permitted to place things that should be in UNSAFE places in SAFE places. They will be used for different reasons, but they definitely also have their use and function.

The opposite doesn't apply. Only drinking resources can also be placed in unsafe passageways (only when combined with providing them in safe places too), which is where the drinking resources will usually be used. Food and litter trays must ALWAYS be in safe places. When this isn't done and they are located in UNSAFE places, problems will arise, of which house soiling issues and fear based issues are the most common.

"We never offer food and drink together. This is incredibly unnatural for the cat, and lowers its motivation to drink."
Anneleen Bru

FOOD & DRINK

Offer food & drink separately

Aha! The cat's most important resource! If we optimise them, they will no longer cause your cat to have sleepless nights. Never place water and food next to each other.

Before you start practically optimising your cat's eating and drinking areas, let's first provide some underlying insights. Predictable resources give cats the option of choice, which creates a sense of peacefulness and control for them. To get to this point, it is best to spend some time experimenting with resources.

This is because there's a good chance your cat was making do with what you'd provided, because it didn't have any other choice before. Insight into the cat's natural instincts will inspire you to try new things out and experiment.

First and foremost, cats rarely catch prey by a pond. The animals they hunt, such as mice, get plenty of moisture from their food, which means they don't have to visit open bodies of water where larger predators, like our cats, go to drink.

In nature, cats don't have a great need to drink either, because they get a lot of moisture from their prey. Both of these mean the location and the manner in which we offer our cat water at home are important.

Cats today must be stimulated to drink water even more, since, more so than before, they need extra water, because they no longer catch live prey, but get dry biscuits instead. The biscuits they eat contain much less moisture (roughly 10%) than, for example, a mouse (70-80%). It's important for your cat's health to drink plenty of water. This is especially true for older cats.

This is why it is not recommended to place food and drink next to each other; something which is evidently still being done by most cat owners. But we eat and drink at the same time, don't we? And don't most bowls consist of two parts - one for water and one for food? Throw it out!

By placing food and drink next to each other, you lower you cat's motivation
to drink, because:

- Cats don't first eat and then drink; they eat and drink at different times.

- Eating is more important for the cat than drinking. So each time your cat goes to the place where the food and drink is gathered, it will choose to eat instead of drinking.

- By placing food and drink close together, cats instinctively sense the water could be polluted, feeling less attracted to drink from the water as a result.

Offering food

Obtaining food is a cat's most important task; it is their top priority. Cats are obligate carnivores, which means they need a lot of protein, which can only be obtained by meat sources, and fat. That's what's in an average prey animal. They don't have much need for fibre - no more than what's in a mouse's stomach - and require almost no carbohydrates.

In nature, cats catch between eight and ten prey animals a day, thus eating multiple small meals every day. As a result, our cats like to visit their bowl ten to twenty times a day to have a little bite to eat. The functioning of a cat's stomach and its digestive system are aligned with this. This makes it very important that we offer the cat this natural eating pattern, in which the cat can control where and how much it eats.

For healthy cats, an ad libitum diet is best (as long as the correct conditions, like multiple eating locations, enrichment, the right diet, and plenty of movement through daily playing, are present).

This means there should always be biscuits present at multiple locations. Only providing one eating location isn't enough, because in nature cats don't consistently find and eat prey in the same location either. Placing food in one location goes against the cat's nature.

Giving your cat the option of having multiple small meals in safe places when it wants to has both physical and mental advantages. The chance of your cat developing FLUTD (feline lower urinary tract disease) decreases, and negative emotions, like frustration and fear, that could result in nervousness and aggressive behaviour, are reduced.

According to the supermarket principle, which works with the n+1 rule, you should always place one more bowl than the number of cats you have.
But there's no harm in placing a few extra bowls. Food is too important! After a while, you can always remove those bowls that are never used.

In principle, most cats won't eat more than they need, so there's no danger of 'overeating'. If your vet has given you a valid reason to no longer offer food ad libitum - because of a medical condition, for example - this should naturally take priority.

However, in practice, I see that owners may think they need to only feed their cat twice a day if their cat is overweight. This could have an adverse effect and could cause your cat to become restless and more fixated on food. We'd rather advise implementing a combination of a natural eating pattern, food enrichment, in which the cat has to work for its daily allowed amount of food, low-caloric food, a lot of playing to burn energy, modifying the environment to stimulate climbing and playing, and have multiple eating locations to make absolutely sure there's no scarcity.

Anti-gobbling bowls

Using anti-gobbling bowls as standard bowls is generally recommendable. This is because cats should have to work for their food. This isn't being mean, but in line with their instinctive behaviour, and therefore perfectly normal. Not all cats immediately grasp the principle, but on average, cats learn quickly.

Anti-gobbling bowls can usually be found in the dog section of the pet shop or online.

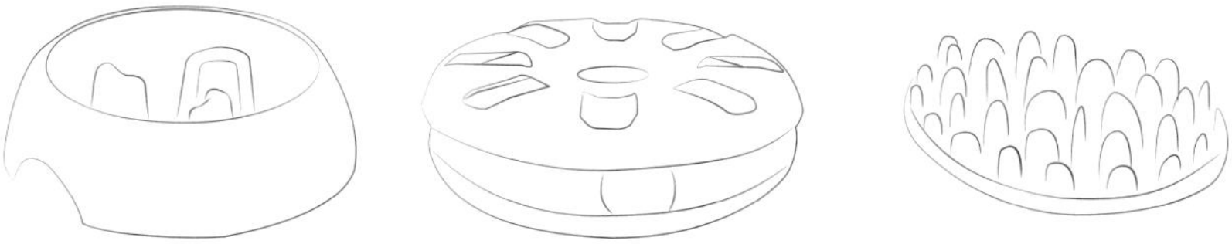

However, if you observe aggression between your cats, make an exception. In such cases, you don't want to further increase the difficulty level of obtaining food. First, the tension between the cats must be resolved. Afterwards, you can make them work for their food.

We must certainly also distinguish between 'fixed' food stations, like the bowls described above, that are always available in the same place and 'mobile' stations, like puzzle feeders. Those puzzle feeders aren't included in the n+1 rule; they're extra.

Offering food

We can use water as a fun way to stimulate natural behaviour. Cats naturally have preferences, but in general, there are a number of things we can take for granted and use as rules of thumb concerning offering drinking resources. Give them a try!

- Place the water far away from the food. As explained previously, cats don't like to drink by their eating bowls. By the way, that's also the reason cats drink from glasses of water, beg by the tap, lick rainwater from the windows or even drink from the toilet.

- Choose to place water bowls in hidden, calm locations, as well as in places along the cat's daily walking routes, like in the hallway, landing and in locations where there is a lot of movement, like the living room.

- Place the water bowl about a foot's distance from the wall, and not against it. Cats will usually prefer to sit between their water bowl and the wall. They feel very vulnerable while they're drinking. In this way, they can look around and keep an eye on the entire space. Cats find the feeling of a wall behind them very soothing as they know nothing can sneak up and surprise them from behind.

- Cats regularly opt for flowing water over stagnant water. Instinctively, they know that stagnant water is riskier, because there could be more bacteria. However, there's no guarantee that they will like water fountains or like them more than water bowls. It's more about the freshness of the water and the playfulness of a jet of water, like when drinking from the tap, for example.

- Cats prefer rainwater and filtered water over tap water. Try collecting some rainwater and take it inside with you. Plenty of rain in our country!

- Avoid plastic bowls; they give the water an unpleasant taste. Rather, use stainless steel, glass, ceramics and so on.

- Cats like large oval or round surfaces, so that their whiskers don't touch the edge of the water source. They don't like that. Their whiskers are very sensitive, remember?

- Either choose high surfaces, like vases (wider at the base than at the mouth for stability but still has a wide surface area to drink from) or items with surface areas of at least eight inches, like salad bowls, vases, soup bowls, and so on. And again: long live IKEA, TK Maxx, ... and the charity shop!

"As carnivores, cats feel very vulnerable when using the litter tray. High time to give them what they need, and that's not a traditional litter tray."
Anneleen Bru

LITTER TRAYS

Litter trays

The litter tray - often discussed, rarely understood. And admittedly, they aren't exactly exciting. Cleaning them or scooping out your cat's business every day is not something many cat owners look forward to. This is exactly why we should look at them more closely. Because there's often a lot of room for improvement.
The litter tray and its use are incredibly important factors in your cat's well-being.

As outlined at the start of this book, domestic cats are descended from an ancestor that used to use the sand plains of North Africa to do its business for thousands of years. There, the soil consists of soft, fine sand, which is ideal for their overly sensitive paws and natural instinct to bury their faeces and urine.

As carnivores, cats produce protein-rich faeces that could potentially attract larger predators. This is precisely why they bury their excrement. Consequently, cats feel exceptionally vulnerable on the litter tray, making it important for all aspects of their toilet to be in order.

Cats' drive towards cleanliness is so strong that they will almost always use the litter tray, even if it is not quite up to scratch - or far from it. But naturally, this shouldn't be a reason not to optimise your cat's litter tray.

Because, if something about the litter tray isn't in order, this could potentially result in house soiling problems, with cats choosing to answer nature's call elsewhere.

In what follows, we will be looking at all aspects that you should take into account when providing litter trays step by step.

Locations

Cats prefer going number one and two in two different locations. This means that if you have one cat, you need at least two litter trays.
Sadly, there's no avoiding this, however much you'd like to, or however much you dislike litter trays. We feel your pain.

Nonetheless, cats will also use just one litter tray for both activities, because of their natural inclination towards hygiene. They have to. Cats are mandatory meat eaters and due to their digestive system, their faeces have a high protein content, which could attract larger predators. This makes it vital for them to bury everything in the right way and in the right place. Only having one litter tray available leaves much to be desired for them, and increases the chance of house soiling problems.

If you have more than one cat, stick to the n+1 rule. Many owners are somewhat startled by this. If you have six cats, for example, according to
this rule, you should place seven litter trays.

Don't panic, because there is a loop hole you can use! You can also work out how many social groups you have, and use that number as 'n', instead of the total number of cats. In principle, this should be enough. But, if house soiling problems still arise, then you should switch to the minimum number of cats you have (=n) +1.

Sizes & types of litter trays

Closed/covered, door on or off? Cat owners' ongoing questions about the litter tray.

Know this, the traditional litter tray you find in most pet shops is a far cry from what your cat would choose for itself. If you still want to use a traditional tray, make sure it's big enough.

That means, at least size XL. The largest you can find in the shop. A litter tray must be at least one and a half times the size of your cat. Don't think twice about removing the little door, because it scrapes against the cat's overly sensitive fur and giving them an extra tap on the bum when entering of exiting the tray, becoming an extra barrier towards the cat wanting to use it.

Whether your cat prefers an open or closed tray is a matter of individual preference. Therefore, it's best to offer both and find out which your cat likes best.

Something that your cat will particularly like is a round, rubber laundry basket without holes in the side and a diameter of roughly 25 inches, or an open storage container without a lid, approximately 30 inches long and 15 inches high.

This is because these boxes have many advantages. Firstly, cats feel much safer due to the high edges, while at the same time being able to keep an eye out for everything happening around them. Leaving the litter tray can be a stressful undertaking for your cat.

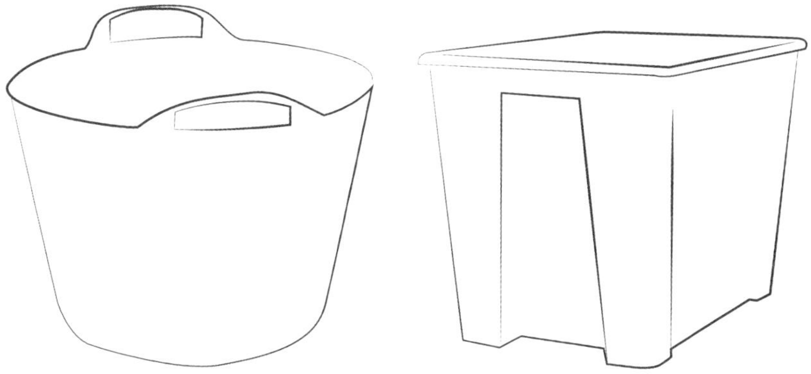

Cats are sometimes harassed by other cats blocking the entrance or jumping on top of the litter tray when they're using it. Because the boxes above are open at the top, the cat can choose from where it wants to leave the tray.

These boxes are also cheap to buy, allowing you to experiment to your heart's content. Even if your cat chooses not to use the box, they are ideal to use as storage containers. Owners also point out that these boxes stand out less, which could encourage owners to place more of them around the house, helping the cats to meet their toilet needs.

It is best not to use these types of high boxes for kittens and senior cats. Their jumping ability isn't good enough. For them, create two different entrances so that they can easily get in and out.

Hygiene

In terms of hygiene, you're absolutely free to treat your cat as a human. We don't like using toilets that contain leftovers from previous visitors either - even more so if they're not our own. Cats feel the same. Although studies have shown that they aren't too concerned with whether the leftovers are their own or someone else's, their presence increases the chance of toilet issues.

Thus, emptying the litter trays every day is of the utmost importance. We know it's no fun... but it's an absolute must!

A tip to make daily scooping easier is to use a litter locker. This is a container to put the dirty, cat sand with clumped-together urine and dried excrement into. The system is comparable to a nappy container for babies.

Using a valve, you let the dirty sand with the cat's leftovers drop into a separate compartment with a biodegradable bag. Using a litter locker (place one next to each litter tray or on every floor at the very least) is hygienic and will save you a lot of time.

Depending on the number of cats you have, tie a knot at the bottom of the compartment once a week, so that it can be disposed of in the garbage without stinking. What a breath of fresh air - both literally and figuratively!

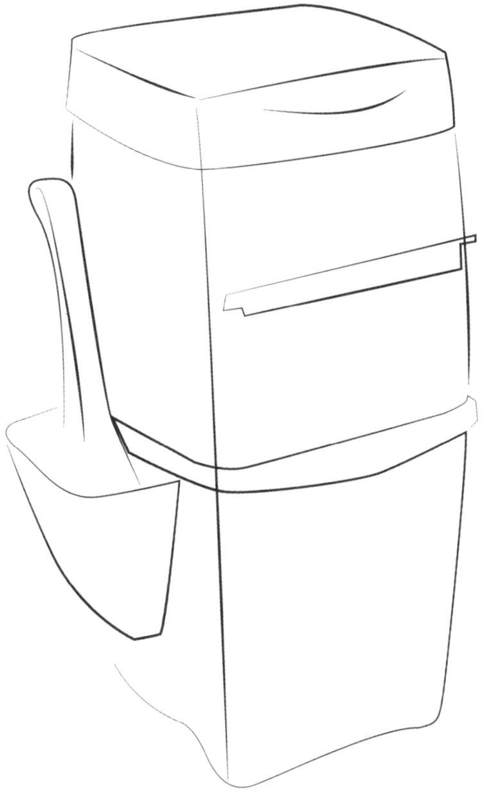

Cat sand

Choosing something in the pet shop is often an impossible task: 'which brand should I choose?' Each bag contains information to convince you, the price is also important, or the biodegradable level, and so on. Everyone has their own motivations.

Let's start with the theory. Cats are descended from the North African savannah. What do we find there? Exactly, fine sand. In combination with the fact that cats have incredibly sensitive paws that function as their sixth sense, this makes the substrate of your cat's litter tray particularly' important.

FACT - This is also the reason why children's sandpits are so popular with neighbourhood cats. They contain fine sand, which feels great on their paws and allows them to bury their business properly.

But what drives the cat towards a certain type of sand? Cats prefer sand that is as much like desert sand as possible. In practice, this is fine cat sand that clumps together - preferably without added smells.

Don't worry if your cat does its business in a litter tray with fine sand and baby perfume; the composition of the sand takes priority.

TIP - In my practice, I witness most house soiling problems among cats that are given wood pellets or other coarse, thick grains (silicate, chalk or quartz) to go to the toilet on. Of course, all facets of the litter tray play a role, but this is something to consider if your cat occasionally urinates outside of the tray.

"Cats must be able to
scratch something
in every area of the house.
It's their most important way to
discharge stress."
Anneleen Bru

SCRATCHING

The scratching cat

Cats scratch for quite a lot of different reasons. Therefore, it's a good idea to provide your cat with opportunities to scratch in each of the three areas of its territory. I always say the following to clients: 'Your cat must be able to see an easily accessible place to scratch in every area of the house.' This also applies to hiding places, by the way, but more about that in a later chapter.

In its core area, close to where it sleeps, the cat scratches to tend to its nails. Cat claws grow from the inside outwards. Scratching helps them to drop old sheaths and keep their claws healthy and sharp. A large, vertical scratching post in the living room is perfect for this. Make sure that these scratching locations are high enough, so that the cat can stretch out completely. Also, make sure the scratching post is sturdy enough, because they often become wobbly after a while.

In its home range, the cat is more likely to scratch to secrete smells to make its environment recognisable, as well as scratching to release stress caused by unfamiliar things or things in the environment it doesn't trust. While the cat won't necessarily be scratching those things themselves, to be able to scratch near them is a very important way to discharge stress. As a result, the need to scratch, and thus to have plenty of scratching opportunities, is much greater if there are strange cats in the house or in the neighbourhood. This is because there are more unknown smells, but also more moments of tension.

Having ample spaces to scratch in this part of its territory enables the cat to empty its stress bucket, preventing the build-up of stress and tension, which could otherwise result in undesirable behaviour, like spraying (a clear stress signal). This makes encouraging scratching behaviour an important part of any therapy plan against spraying, because it discharges stress and gives the cat the chance to secrete pheromones and deal with its environment.

In practice, I find that cats prefer to scratch on horizontal surfaces to discharge stress. Additionally, scientific studies indicate that cats prefer to scratch on wavy surfaces, in the shape of a flattened, half-eight shape. In today's market, there are numerous brands that sell wavy items of scratching furniture that are just wide enough for the cat to scratch, so that you can easily place them in a passageway.

	Core Area	Home Range	Hunting Area
Claw care	•		
Back stretching (after sleeping)	•		
Leaving scratch marks (visual marking)		•	•
Secreting pheromones		•	•
Discharging stress	• (when in danger)	•	•
Attracting attention	•	•	

"Cats literally
think: 'If I
can't see you,
you can't see
me.'
So the golden
rule is: If you
cannot look your
cat in the eye,
pretend like it
doesn't exist.
Works miracles
with your cat!"
Anneleen Bru

HIDING PLACES

See which way the cat jumps

It is a broadly known fact that cats are tree climbers. They love to be up high to keep an eye on everything. They perceive the world in 3D. High places are like extra 'apartments' for them in the house; places they can use as part of their home range or core area.

Instinctively, they not only want to keep a lookout (which, by the way, is vital for them); elevated perches are also very handy to bring yourself to safety, both in anticipation of a predator or in the actual presence of a predator.

Cats feel less stressed when observing threats from high places than when they're standing eye to eye with them. The mere presence of high places generates a sense of calm, regardless of whether they're actually being used. 'Because, if something should happen, I could escape *there*, *there* or *on top of that*.'

But what's the truth of the matter? Over the years, I have visited hundreds of cat owners and found that every square inch of high areas in and around their homes are filled with junk (have a look at your own home). ☺ Cats are either not allowed to make use of them (kitchen counter, dining tables, coffee tables, sofas, and so on), or their access to them is incredibly unpredictable (sometimes they are things placed there, sometimes there aren't, sometimes they're allowed to go on them, sometimes they aren't...).

Thus, with the exception of that one scratching post somewhere in a corner, cats often lack access to consistently reachable and reliable high areas within their environments.

EXERCISE - Get a large laundry basket or box and empty ALL high places in your living room (cupboards, shelf space, racks in wardrobes, dressers, in and on coffee tables, and so on). Leave them cleared for six weeks and find out which of these your cats like to use. Lay down fleece blankets, treats and toys as reminders.

Also create extra support tools, like small steps and intermediate levels with racks, stacked boxes or cat towers, for easy access. Older and more easily frightened cats will be very thankful for this.

Staring & visual barriers

Staring is a form of self-defence among cats that want to scare away a threat from a distance. As solitary hunters, it's important not to get hurt. Understandably, they prefer to solve issues at a distance.
Two cats who are 'looking' (staring) at each other, are usually really fighting. A conflict that escapes the average cat owner.

With this insight in the back of our minds, it is best to create as many visual barriers as possible in your home, which cats can use to hide behind and potentially escape threatening situations. Ignorance is bliss, so to speak.

Because cats always think: 'If I can't see you, you can't see me.' Remember? Even if your cat's tail or back is sticking out from behind the table leg, it still thinks you can't see it.

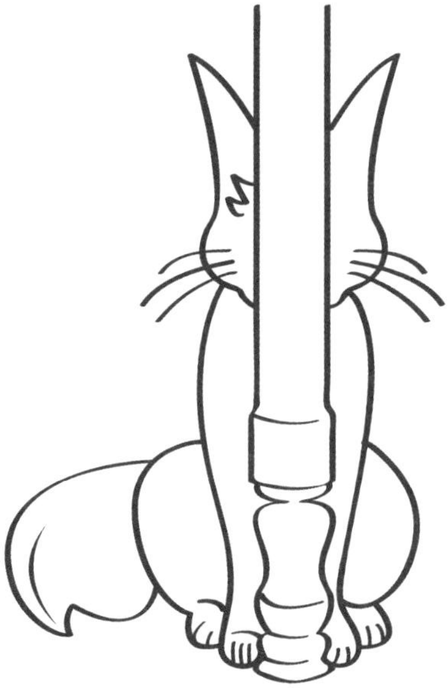

Therefore, some important and useful tips concerning hiding places for your cats!

Never look your cat straight in the eyes.

Always drop your eyes softly to tell it everything is okay.

If you cannot look your cat in the eye, pretend like it doesn't exist.

Place cardboard boxes with multiple entrances in both safe and unsafe places, so that your cat can always hide first, before adopting other techniques to chase off enemies.

Do you have windows that reach down to the floor? Cover the bottom part with soft, removable solid opaque foil. Start at the floor. The width of the roll is usually sufficient, since you will already have reached the height at which cats can see each other through the window. Foil on the window might not be the most aesthetic solution, but it is definitely the best and cheapest. Your cat will be eternally grateful.

Because even though you rarely see neighbour cats in your garden, these cats are often quite aware of whether you're at home, and will wait patiently to drop by after you're gone. Closing the curtains isn't enough in such cases, because it's unpredictable.

EXERCISE - Take three cardboard boxes of roughly 12 by 16 inches (30 by 40 cm) and create holes that your cat can fit through in three of the sides of the boxes. Cats prefer 'mouse holes' that start at the floor and are shaped like half circles. Place the boxes in three important passageways or open places at home and test whether they are being used for six weeks.

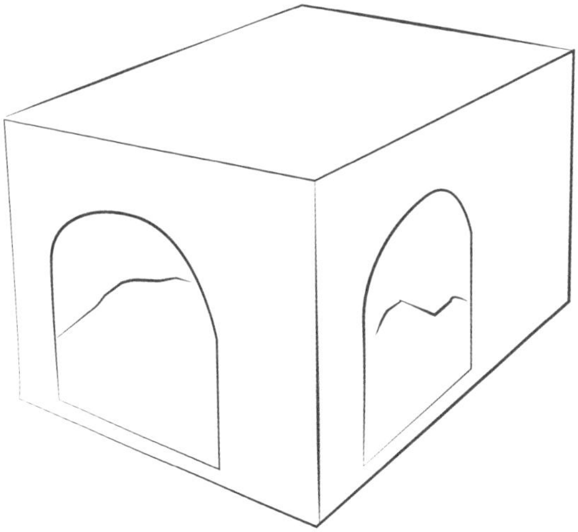

What about sleeping places?

When cat owners ask me about the best sleeping place for a cat, I always advise them to follow their cat's lead. This is because cats select their own sleeping places based on safety and availability and what their territory looks like at that time.

TIP - If you still want to buy a cat bed, make sure it has multiple entrances, so that your cat always feels like it can escape through more than one exit and can also keep an eye out in multiple directions.

Follow your cat where it likes to sleep and lay down a fleece blanket. Not necessarily for your cat, because it will also sleep without a blanket, but mostly as a reminder to yourself not to clutter your cat's favourite sleeping place, thereby making it unavailable and unpredictable. One of the best things you can do for your cats and their sleeping place is to respect the places where they choose to sleep by completely ignoring them when they're sleeping or resting somewhere.

TIP - Cats prefer to sleep on straight, horizontal or hanging (slightly concave) surfaces. Many cat baskets are actually dog baskets with a ridge and a convex cushion in the middle. These basket don't 'hang' - quite the opposite. Cats don't like these convex sleeping surfaces.

Pretending like they're sleeping.

'Fake sleepers' are sometimes seen in larger groups (shelters, breeders, cat hotels), in which some cats experience difficulty with tension and the scarcity of available resources.

The only way for them to deal with these situations is to pretend like they're sleeping. 'Fake sleeping' is their last form of escape.

Without this background knowledge, it may appear like these cats spend a lot of time sleeping, but they spend much less time in REM states of sleep.

And this is precisely the part of the deep sleep phase you need to dream (even though it has not yet been proven that cats dream), so that your body can process what you experienced during the day.

When cats pretend to be sleeping, but are actually sleeping a lot less, this wreaks havoc on their mental and physical well-being.

TIP - You can test whether your cat is sleeping by simply snapping your fingers and observing its response. Do the ears respond? If so, your cat isn't sleeping deeply. Cats in REM sleep also display brief twitches, 'like they're chasing a mouse in their dreams'.

FACT - You can recognise a cat that's pretending to sleep or which isn't sleeping deeply by its posture. It's sitting in a crouched position with its eyes closed, its ears rotated and its whiskers pressed against its cheeks.

A cat that is sleeping deeply will sleep on its back or on its side, with
ears pointing forward, occasionally displaying small twitches that indicate it's in the REM sleep phase.

Never disrupt these cats. It's extremely disconcerting to them. This is because animals are very vulnerable when they're asleep.

Enrichment for your cats

"The need for cats to hunt is not proportionate to how hungry they feel. Cats have to hunt, and if you don't stimulate that instinct, they will find another way."
Anneleen Bru

HUNTING BEHAVIOUR

Cats are born solitary hunters. This means they are entirely self-dependent when it comes to obtaining food.

Their solitary hunting behaviour has resulted in well-developed superpowers, like exceptional hearing, a phenomenal sense of smell, sharp and quick claws and a body that is equipped entirely to obtain information from its environment.

The cat's instinct to hunt is not proportionate to how hungry it feels. This means that they feel the need to hunt, regardless of whether they're hungry. Of course, there is a relationship between their hunting behaviour and hunger; cats will hunt more when they're hungry, and also try to catch more prey. But the urge to hunt - the hunting instinct - still exists even if the cat isn't hungry.

Cats are opportunistic hunters. Thus, cats will hunt whenever the opportunity presents itself. Their instinct is stronger than they are.

Studies have shown that cats will leave prey that they've caught lying when they spot another prey animal to chase! The advantage of catching a second prey animal is larger than the risk of the first catch being pinched. This increases the chance of sufficient food, and possible even two catches.

TIP - Because their hunting instinct is stronger than they are, it is important to be careful not to tire cats out when playing with them. They can't simply say 'enough' and walk away. That would go against their natural instinct too much. As long as their prey is moving, they have to keep chasing.
When a cat is panting, you've clearly gone too far. You need to prevent that from happening.

Gifts?

Cats hunt in the hunting area and living range of their territory, but prefer to eat their prey in the safe environment of their core area. This is why you might see your cat walking off to another room with a toy, treat or prey, or bring prey that it has caught outside into the house or leave dead prey on the doormat. The cat didn't eat its prey because it wasn't hungry. As responsible owners, we give our cats plenty of food and extras, right?

FACT - Cats leaving mice lying around the house aren't leaving you gifts. Rather, they bring them into their core area, because this is where they'd usually eat their prey in peace. Other older studies point out that leaving behind prey is a corrupted form of maternal behaviour, in which the cat brings dead or half-dead prey animals into its core area like a mother wanting to teach her kittens to hunt. As you can see, there are multiple opinions concerning this phenomenon.

On average, a well-fed domestic cat spends around five hours a day hunting. That's quite a long period they spend searching for, staring at, spying on, stalking, jumping on, biting, plucking skin/feathers and eventually eating prey.

TIP - Realising your cat needs to be stimulated daily in its hunting behaviour (by offering something that moves on its own accord that the cat can spy on, chase, catch, lick, bite and kick) is the first step in the right direction of offering your cat the proper enrichment to increase and maintain its happiness.

Cats have flexible schedules, depending on the availability of prey in their territories. As such, they're usually active during dawn in the morning and dusk at night, and will hunt more at night in summer and during the daytime in winter.

As we have already extensively pointed out in previous chapters, cats aren't concerned with the colour of their toys or of prey (although their contrast with the background can play a role).

Pet shops mostly offer these colourful toys in all shapes and sizes because they attract people!
Factors that are important to cats are the smells, movements and sounds of potential prey, and to succeed in the hunt.

"Cats aren't lazy; you just
haven't found out what
they truly enjoy playing
with. So, you've got some
homework to find out."
Anneleen Bru

TYPES OF PLAY

There are three types of play for cats that we should know and take into consideration. Cats are opportunistic hunters that need to be challenged.

Social play

Cats playing rough and tumble together are using play to practice for the 'real' thing, like fighting and hunting. Play is considered a type of affiliative behaviour and is observed throughout the cat's life. Even in unusual situations, such as between unneutered tomcats in a situation of food scarcity. In such situations, play doesn't appear to be evolutionarily viable. Nevertheless, researchers assume there must be an underlying reason why play still occurs.

Playing is good for the cat's well-being, to discharge energy and to strengthen its social relationships with other cats.

Locomotory play

Locomotory play means playing with the environment. Jumping, climbing, scratching and walking are examples of playing with the environment and are good for the cat and its health. Owners regularly say their cats have a 'wild five minutes', running through the house like maniacs. This is a good example of locomotory play. Thus, make sure your cats have sufficient space and opportunities to do this and display this kind of behaviour. It is important for them and their well-being.

TIP - You can stimulate locomotory play by combining it with predatory play. Lure the cat to different heights using a rod to release extra energy.

Predatory play behaviour

Of course, this type of play is the most well known, but it is still often underestimated and underexploited by owners. The toys you find in the shop are usually not really attuned to what cats truly enjoy and require to discharge their hunting energy. As an example, your cat doesn't care what shape or colour toys have, but that doesn't stop manufacturers from using them to make them appealing to us. As previously explained, cats are mostly concerned with the smell of the toy (synthetic or made from organic or animal material), which sound it makes (fluttering) and whether it moves (moving away from the cat, like prey trying to escape).

A small, red, synthetic mouse lying on the floor motionlessly isn't very interesting to most cats, and could possible even be a let-down. This is because motionless prey goes against everything cats need to hunt. There are cats that will try to get the 'dead' toy moving, but, although laudable of them, is quite sad from a behavioural perspective.

We don't watch a television that's switched off, do we?

As a result, there are many people who think their cat doesn't like to play, is spoilt, is being difficult or is simply lazy. But there is a hunter in each of them! You simply have to know how to get it out. And for this you must experiment, experiment, experiment!

Predatory play behaviour itself is divided into three phases:

1) hunting their prey (movement)
2) weakening and biting their prey to death (smells)
3) eating their prey (food)

To find out which phase your cat enjoys most, it is important to allow it to explore all phases of predatory play behaviour.

There are cats that prefer movement, while others prefer smells in a prey they can kick with their back legs. There are also cats that, within their preference for moving prey, express a clear preference for birds (feathers, fluttering, in the air) and not for mice (fur, crawling, on the ground), for example. There are also cats that like small insects flying away at eye level.

There are numerous variations within the first 'moving' phase that you can try out at different ages to find out what triggers your cat most.

Sadly, most cats are never given the chance to find out what they truly enjoy hunting, because owners don't experiment with things or don't understand what's at the root of their hunting instinct. Hopefully, this chapter will have changed that. Do you understand now why so many cats are 'lazy', or appear to be?

HOMEWORK - Find different types of animal material - like fur, feathers or wool (obtained responsibly) and test different sizes and smells. What is (are) your cat's favourite(s)?

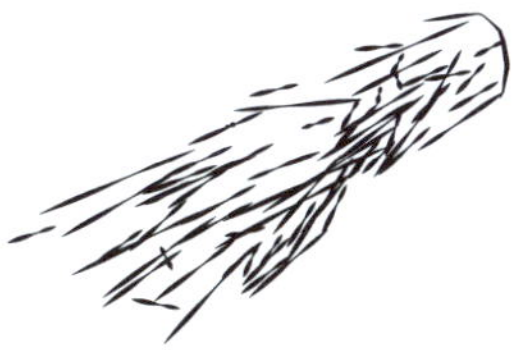
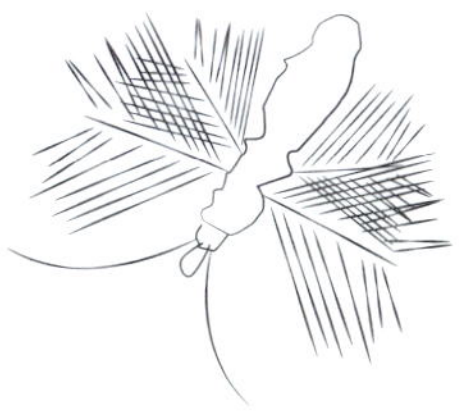
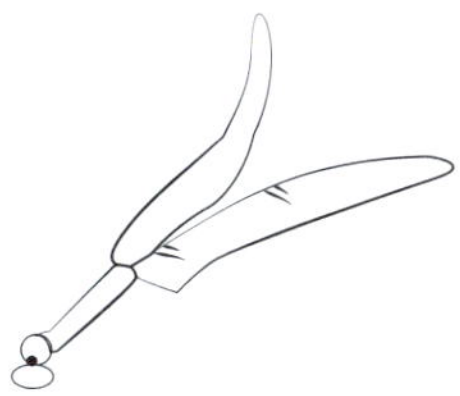

"Cats experience prey habituation, which means they no longer play with something they've already 'killed'. So, tidy up your living room."

Anneleen Bru

ENRICHMENT FOR YOUR CAT

Enrichment for cats

Enrichment is intended to stimulate natural behaviour among animals. In the first place, this encompasses ALL behaviour, including eating, drinking, toileting, hiding places, and so on. This means you can stimulate all forms of behaviour.
In this chapter, we will discuss how and why we do which things to stimulate the natural hunting behaviour of our cats.

Not stimulating cats' hunting behaviour can generate a considerable number of problems, like listlessness, social tension, obesity, emotions of frustration, numerous undesirable forms of behaviour - like climbing in curtains, scratching, aggression towards the owner, stalking and attacking other cats, excessive scratching, spraying, fearful behaviour and even house soiling problems.

Therefore, it's not only important to provide hunting enrichment within a therapeutic context, but also as a tool to prevent unwanted behaviour.

Practical information while hunting

Cats like to hide and scratch while hunting.
It is a way for them to instantly discharge stress, because hunting sessions are quite demanding on their bodies.
On top of that, the alertness required to hunt is like an explosion within the cat's sensory system. In such situations, it likes to sit inside a box or under a chair, and likes to have a cardboard scratching board nearby.
Additionally, cats also experience sensory 'prey habituation'.

This means that if they encounter lifeless prey on the ground, they will experience it as something they recently killed already. Instinctively, they will think something isn't right ('wasn't my attack successful?') and ignore the prey.

Now that we know this, it's actually quite hilarious how often toys are left lying around their living room. For people, it's a mess, and cats barely play with them because of this prey habituation. There's also often a box with toys, 'so that the cat can choose its own toy'.

This might work for a child or a dog, but certainly not for a cat. That's because cats want to be triggered by something new (a small change is enough) and by things that move 'on their own accord', without them having to set them into motion.

TIP - Use a box with toys from which you take toys and offer them to your cat, thereby alternating between them. Your cat will experience toys as new prey. Is it done playing with a toy? Remove the toy, put it back in the toy box and leave a few toys lying around in other places throughout the house. This is a fun way for them to continue to hunt, especially when you're not at home or asleep. By alternating sufficiently, the same toys can nonetheless give the cat the feeling that it's encountering new prey.

Solitary hunters!

We cannot emphasise the fact that cats are solitary hunters enough. Therefore, let them play solitarily, which means all by themselves. Cats don't need each other to catch prey. It's as simple as that.

Owners often play with groups of cats, in which usually the most confident (not the most 'dominant', because there's no such thing as dominance among cats, remember?) will chase the prey, and the rest will look on from a distance like wallflowers, because they don't want to enter into conflict with one another.

In reality, all of the cats would like to chase the prey, but they aren't given the chance. This results in owners who think they are playing with their cats enough and that these cats simply don't feel like playing. While actually, these cats aren't playing enough and become deprived.

The three hunting phases

In my practice, I use a simple representation for cats' hunting phases. This representation shows how we can stimulate each part, allowing the cat to express its instinctive nature.

CATCHING

- Sitting and waiting
- Exploring
- Investigating the environment
- Watching/staring
- Finding prey
- Chasing prey

KILLING

- Raking with hind legs
- Biting the prey
- Licking the prey
- Releasing the prey and catching it again
- Throwing prey in the air

CONSUMING

- Eating
- Burying

These three phases can subsequently be subdivided into three types of enrichment:

1. HUNTING ENRICHMENT
2. OLFACTOR ENRICHMENT
3. FOOD ENRICHMENT

Hunting enrichment

In the first phase, we stimulate the cat by offering movement, emphasising hunting prey, WITHOUT catching it.

Here, a long rod is best (roughly one yard (metre) in length), because this will prevent the cat from realising you're controlling the toy. The cat must be able to chase something to hunt. You have to experiment with this a little, because all cats have their own preferences, which, additionally, can change throughout their lifetimes.

Some cats prefer moving prey on the ground; others prefer airborne prey. One cat might prefer birds, while another cat prefers small insects or mouse-shaped objects. Some cats like tiny items, like hair bands or fake spiders, while others prefer to chase larger prey. Try to find out what your cat prefers and continue to experiment throughout its life.

The prey's structure is also important here. Cats prefer living prey, so try to work with structures that are as lifelike as possible; soft toys, artificial and real fur.

Make sure when using fur toys, that they have been obtained in an ecological and responsible manner, and are from western countries. This increases the chance that the animal from which the fur has been obtained had a free-roaming life. These furs will predominantly have been obtained through hunting, as road kills or as residual or by-product of the meat industry. This means these animals are not specifically bred, kept and killed to function as cat toys.

TIP - Toys by Purrs are handmade, and offer a wide range of different animal furs - like sheep, buffalo, hare and feathers - to experiment with, optionally in combination with valerian. The rod imitates a real fluttering bird, with sound. Are you already using them for your cat? Absolutely brilliant to see your cat jump and play!
www.purrsinourhearts.co.uk

Smell enrichment

In the second hunting phase, the cat starts to 'rake', falling onto its side, grasping the prey with her front paws and raking it with its hind legs, while licking and biting the prey at the same time.

In addition to being instinctive hunting behaviour, this is also an important way for the cat to discharge stress, and we can stimulate this behaviour using smells.

Catnip is the most well-known method of smell enrichment for cats. It has an invigorating effect, but is still often overestimated. This is because it is genetically determined whether a cat will respond to it. Fifty to 70 percent of cats are able to respond to it; the others aren't. Sadly, almost all toys in the pet shop are drenched in catnip to make them 'interesting'. But this only works for around half of all cats.

TIP - Make sure you use catnip from the USA or Canada. They have the best quality.

Valerian is an excellent product to use with cats. Especially cats having a hard time will benefit from it. That's because a cat's stress level determines how fiercely it will respond to it. Dried valerian root has a stimulating effect while the cat plays with it. But, in the hours that follow, it has a calming effect on the cat, while also improving the cat's resilience.

TIP - Use valerian daily in different toys, especially among cats in need of extra stimulation, such as apartment cats and fearful and spraying cats. Moreover, valerian toys are easy to make yourself. Just fill a small sock with 10 grams of valerian (purchasable online or at the better health food shops) and toilet paper or cotton to fill it up, and then tie a knot in it.

Make sure to take away toy cushions with valerian when the cat's done with them. Alternate toys and place new toys in other places around the house, so that the cat can run into them unexpectedly. 'Oh look! Prey!' Mainly offer the toys when you're not at home or asleep.

TIP - Put all mice and balls you have at home in a properly sealed storage jar with one hundred grams of dried valerian root and/or catnip. This will keep strengthening the smell of the toys.

Food enrichment

As previously discussed, making your cat work for its food is an absolute must. There are different methods and levels with which you can build up and experiment with food enrichment.

Food enrichment can be divided into static and mobile stations. Static eating locations are covered by our n+1 rule, and should always be in the same place and filled with biscuits.

These food sources must remain predictable for the cat.

Examples of these are anti-gobbling bowls or 'slow down bowls', and thinking toys that require a cat to use its paws and its brain to get to its food. You can also use toys that aren't originally intended as food bearers, but are perfectly suitable to be used in that way.

Mobile stations are eating opportunities that you supply as extras, and which you can provide to offer the cat extra stimulation when you're away, for example. Homemade food toys like filled egg cartons and toilet roles are fun and cheap!

On top of that, we're also fans of experimenting with feeder balls! But not all items on the market are equally suitable for cats. Many balls are too heavy, because they're originally intended for dogs, only have one hole, thereby frustrating for the cat, and have raised parts or studs that make too much noise when they roll on the floor.

TIP - The PetSafe Slimcat feeder ball has been our absolute favourite for years!

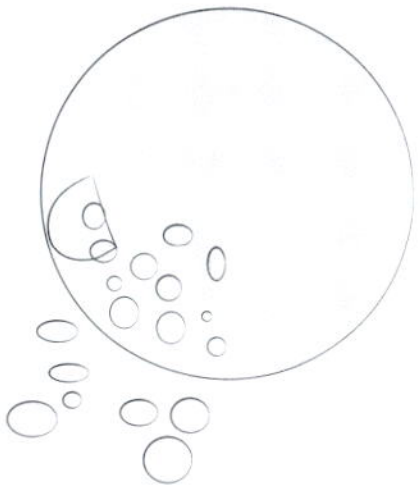

"Your cat is not lazy;
you're just playing with it
in the wrong way."
Anneleen Bru

DOS & DON'TS WHILE PLAYING

Don'ts while playing

- Not playing daily.
- Playing until the cat is panting.
- Only trying something one time and drawing incorrect conclusions too quickly.
- Playing with the hand, fingers, toes and/or foot.
- Making your cat set something into motion itself.
- Leaving toys lying around.
- Concluding your cat doesn't like to play.
- Having insufficient variation/novelty in what you provide.
- Using frustrating toys that the cat cannot catch (such as laser pens, games on the iPad).
- Only stimulating one phase of the hunt.
- Only stimulating one type of play.
- Playing with multiple cats at the same time.

Dos while playing

- Stimulating the hunting instinct three to five times a day - a few minutes is enough!
- Stimulating the three different hunting phases (play, smells, food) and finding out which phase(s) your cat prefers (be aware that preferences can change over time).
- Playing with your cat alone; individual play without other cats (solitary hunter).
- Not exhausting your cat. The impulse to hunt is stronger than the cat itself.
- Varying in terms of frequency, novelty, location and intensity.
- Movement and smells (herbs, animal materials, items from nature) are important.
- Not leaving prey lying around.
- Creating distance between you and the cat, so that you don't get in its way or run the risk of getting hurt, and the cat can do its own thing undisturbed.
- Don't encourage the cat all the time. The hunting game is something the cat must do on its own (solitary hunter), and therefore not always quality time between human and animal.
- Some cats have the need to 'run through' the hunting process entirely and cover the three hunting phases. If this is the case for your cat, provide it with prey that has an animal smell that it can rake and/or give the cat a treat at the end of the hunting game.
- Beware of labelling cats as 'lazy'! All cats must be able to hunt, since they all have the same natural hunting instinct. Some cats may be fiercer than others, and thus there are differences in the hunting opportunities they require.

Improving your relationship with your cat

"Our way of showing love is very threatening for a cat. If in nature a large creature comes walking up to you while staring, you'd best start walking!"

Anneleen Bru

DISPLAYING AFFECTION

Differences between cats and humans

Cats and humans have completely different ways of showing affection to each other. By understanding where they are different, we can adapt and improve our relationship with our cat. The cat will feel more at ease and seek out contact more. Fun for both, right?

Ways of showing affection that cats (usually) don't like?

- Cuddling
- Picking up
- Holding like a baby
- Stroking
- Kissing
- Talking to the cat
- Searching for and approaching the cat
- Comforting the cat
- Placing the cat on your lap and keeping it there

Ways in which cats show their affection which are (usually) misunderstood by their owners?

- Dry spraying (quivering the tail without urine)
  Showing its rear end/flank upon greeting
- Coming close to its owner
- Lying close to its owners
- Slowly blinking both eyes
- Yawning (when they haven't just woken up)
- Wagging the tip of its tail slowly
- Displaying its belly
- Biting softly/little bites (beware, this could also mean irritation)

If we look at the different sides of the story, we see a lot of misinterpretations in practice, which could easily and quickly be solved with more insight. Owners who really like seeing their cat often wonder what they can do to make their cat want to see them more.

Moreover, some cats that like to be around their owners sometimes start becoming tense or displaying aggressive behaviour, like striking out when they're being stroked, even if they themselves were the ones seeking out affection!

Let's discuss a few examples that will be recognisable to many owners.

Cats showing their affection by displaying their rear end. In their world, this is non-threatening behaviour through which to display trust and invite affection. That's why we're often so successful with our cats when we really don't have time for them and would prefer it if they left us alone, like when we're trying to reach a deadline or are reading the newspaper. By ignoring the cat, we're actually telling the cat in its language that we like seeing it and would like to cuddle. This the same reason why people who really don't like cats very much always seem to attract them. They intentionally ignore them to keep them away, but, as a result, these are exactly the people cats like to sit with and cuddle. They display precisely that behaviour (ignoring, not giving attention, not stroking) that cats perceive to be friendly, inviting and safe.

Cats have a deeply ingrained instinct that tells them that in nature, a large animal approaching them with its eyes wide open (which is exactly what people do when they think something, like a pet or a baby, is cute) is best avoided and given an as wide berth as possible. Large, wide-eyed animals or excited owners are terribly threatening to them. Firstly, we should be and remain aware of this.

Like all other animals and small children, cats literally think: 'If I can't see you, then you can't see me.' Usually, when we cannot look directly into our cats eyes, it's possible that she is hiding and she thinks that we can't see her. As a result, we could be causing our cat stress every time we then seek her out, call out for her or stroke her when we can't make eye contact. This is because our behaviour seems highly unpredictable and unexpected to the cat, because it thinks we don't know where she is.

"However well you know your cat, always allow it to smell your hand before you stroke it. Always!"
Anneleen Bru

MAKING CONTACT WITH YOUR CAT

Too much love isn't good for your cat

Cats are free animals that value control over their situation enormously, and this also applies to their bodies.

In practice, we see that kittens, depending on their socialisation with humans, that were entirely subjected to the cuddling frenzy of their human family members have switched to a form of learned helplessness. This means that over the years they have learned that there's nothing they can do against it, so they should simply submit to the experience.
This helpless feeling primarily arises among cats that are continuously lifted up, held like a baby or sought out when they're quietly sleeping or resting. Their lack of response doesn't mean they're okay with it - quite the opposite. The cat still experiences physical stress, but doesn't have any way to resist it.

It is important to be aware of this as cat owners. People's understanding needs to be enhanced in order the optimise the cat's well being. Forcing your cat to lie still like a baby creates a deep sense of unrest in your cat, even if that unrest isn't visible. That unrest could result in a broader feeling of fear and result in undesirable behaviour.

FACT - Forcing your cat to lie still like a baby creates a deep sense of unrest in your cat.

We are going to discuss a general technique which I am convinced is experienced positively by all cats - happy or fearful, young or old - because the cat can choose safe contact with its owner. We have had amazing results with it in practice.

Making contact with your cat

Employ this technique with your own cats, but also with cats you don't know. Your cats aren't the only cats that deserve to be treated respectfully and greeted just because you know them.

TIP - Use this technique for four weeks with cats that are very fearful, and you will notice an enormous improvement by creating predictability in the cat's experience. It is also absolutely worth the effort to adapt your behaviour with cats that appear happy, and seeing how they respond. Try it!

1. Stick your hand out about eight inches from your body. This is an invitation for the cat to carefully sniff it. Most cats will really enjoy the invitation and approach you quickly.

2. As the cat is smelling your hand, there are three possible outcomes. It is important to know what they are and to respond appropriately!

Scenario A - The cat smells your hand and rubs the side of its chin against your hand. The cat turns 90° and shows its side or rear. You're allowed to make contact with the cat. The best way is by briefly scratching the cat's chin, the corners of its mouth, or behind its ears. Stay away from the rest of the cat's body, unless you are completely sure the cat enjoys this - if the animal was highly socialised to this from an early age, for example.

Scenario B - The cat smells your hand but remains at a distance of a few inches. The cat isn't rubbing your hand, but it isn't walking away either. This is the first signal that thing aren't fine. You mustn't touch the cat, but you can make contact by slowly dropping your eyes (blinking both eyes) and softly talking to the cat.

Scenario C - The cat sniffs your hand and looks away or walks away. Don't touch the cat, and leave the animal alone. We recommend not talking either. The cat doesn't feel comfortable with what it smelt, and we must respect that.

3. By always doing this when you make contact, you will see that the cat learns that you, as the owner, visitor or carer, are always predictable, and that it has a choice in the situation.

The cat will be thankful of this and (want to) make contact more often.

"How can you get your cat to like being around you more? Ignore it. Yes, ignore – really ignore – the cat."

Anneleen Bru

IGNORE,
IGNORE,
IGNORE!

Why ignoring works

Ignoring is actually doing nothing; not giving the cat any attention. So simple, and yet so difficult! Why is it so difficult for us to keep our hands off those fluffy critters?

Ignoring it is the best tool to develop a good relationship with your cat. Leaving cats alone and letting them do their thing gives them a feeling of calmness and confidence. This leads to a sense of control over the situation and allows them to decide whether they want contact.

For many owners, ignoring is apparently a relative concept that has many variants. Nonetheless, ignoring is very simple. It means 'pretending like your cat doesn't exist', or simply, 'not doing anything'. So, no looking, no talking, no calling, no stroking, no seeking your cat out, no touching, no picking up, and so on. Not doing anything; simply doing nothing with your cat.

We distinguish between two types of ignoring that you as the owner can do.

1. Passive ignoring

Passive ignoring means staying in the same place and position, but no longer giving any attention to your cat, by looking away or turning your body, for example. But what exactly do we want to passively ignore? Well, first and foremost, the presence of the cat. But also, any form of instinctive, natural behaviour. Easier said than done.

I have a golden rule here. If you cannot look into your cat's eyes, pretend like the cat doesn't exist. It's that simple! Is the cat sleeping, lying under or behind something, in another space or does it have its back turned towards you? All moments in which you cannot look the cat in the eyes, causing the cat to literally think you cannot see it nor reach it. In that sense, ignoring is very respectful in the animal world and contrasts with our human habits and standards of politeness.

In addition, we also want to passively ignore any form of natural behaviour, like exploring, eating, drinking, hunting, playing, toileting, looking around, hiding, and so on. Here, also pretend like your cat doesn't exist. Your cat doesn't need you when its going about its natural cat behaviour. Without us realising it, disturbing the cat can cause countless moments of stress.

2. Active ignoring

Active ignoring means getting up calmly and going to another room, to get a cup of coffee or to use the toilet, for example. By removing yourself from the situation, you give the cat the chance to relax entirely.

So what exactly will we be actively ignoring? All subtle and clear signs of stress. Whatever you are doing, whether to do with the cat or not, just stand up and walk away. Your cat will instantly breathe a sigh of relief.

"Resocialisation training works
wonders for cats having
a hard time around us."
Anneleen Bru

RESOCIALISING SCARED CATS

Training your cat & letting it relax

In this chapter, we will explore a training technique to let timid, shy and mildly scared cats know everything is okay and that they can feel at ease. This does not occur automatically, since we both speak entirely different languages. Over the years, I have increasingly returned to this training technique, because it generates truly amazing results. When combined with a considerable degree of patience, of course.

The training technique is explained in four steps, of which the first two are effective trainings, and the following two can be implemented in daily life. People with experience with clicker training will notice that this technique is a simple version of classical and operant conditioning that generates strong results.

Preparation & equipment

Find something your cat really enjoys, like a treat, fresh meat or a fluid snack. Make sure you can give it quickly and efficiently. Scared cats don't like eating from your hand, so place it in front of them or use a spoon for wet food. Stroking or talking to scared cats are not good rewards.

Choose suitable locations and times for your training moments, in which your cat is entirely at ease.
Thus, you should follow your cat's pace. You will also need a sound, like the short double clicking sound you make with your tongue.

Preferably, this is a sound your cat isn't familiar with yet, and which you haven't used before. It is also important that the sound itself doesn't cause the cat to become scared.

Step 1 - Click = reward

We are going to make the sound into a reliable predictor of tasty cat treats, so that the clicking sound becomes valuable, something the cat wants to hear and which makes it feel good. Sit in front of the cat calmly and without moving. Make sure there are no distractions around. Subsequently, make a clicking sound with your tongue and give the cat a treat. The only behaviour your cat has to display is to be calm and stay near you. In this way, the cat remains conscious of what is happening and can anticipate the treat when it hears the clicking sound. Repeat this roughply 20 times per training Repeat this roughly 20 times, although it depends on the individual cat so adjust accordingly and train one to two times a day.

Take your time to establish a positive association between the clicking sound and giving the cat the treat. Repeat step 1 for at least one week and test throughout whether your cat responds when it's looking away, for example, and you make the clicking sound. If the cat looks up without you moving your hand to give it a treat, you know it's starting to understand. Remember that this is an unconscious process for the cat that requires time! We want to programme this thoroughly.

Step 2 - Cat is happy -> click -> reward = what you're doing now is great!

Spread a number of jars with cat treats throughout the house, so that you can easily reach them wherever you are. You have some time between making the clicking sound and giving the treat, because you have trained thoroughly to create the positive association. But make sure you don't have to go or walk too far to get to the jar with treats.

In step 2, start rewarding all forms of desirable behaviour in the house by clicking. What is desirable behaviour? Any form of behaviour that you as the owner or carer want to see more of in the future; when the cat comes towards you, is calm, looks at you, enters confidently, jumps on the sofa with you, and so on.

If you make the clicking sound when the cat is showing desirable behaviour and subsequently give the cat a treat, you're actually telling the cat in clear language: 'Yes, well done. What you're doing now and how you're feeling is what I want to see'. Without wasting any words.

Firstly, this teaches the cat that what it was doing before results in a reward, causing it to occur more frequently in the future as a result. In the theory, this is called 'Thorndike's law of effect'. Secondly, you are creating an association between your cat's happy and confident behaviour and the clicking sound (and the reward that always follows). And we will need this in the following phase and steps.

Repeat this step throughout the day whenever you see your cat displaying desired behaviour for a period of three to four weeks. This will allow the association to become deeply ingrained at an unconscious level.

Step 3 - Comfort your cat - 'there is no danger'

This is where things become exciting. You have spent four weeks teaching your cat that whenever it hears a clicking sound it gets a reward if it's at ease. You have associated the sound with a positive feeling. We're now going to encourage that feeling to arise at times when the cat is unjustifiably not feeling entirely safe. This teaches your cat that it is actually allowed to feel secure, safe and at ease, because there's no danger lurking.

Of course, your cat doesn't know that yet. But you are going to assist, guide and coach it. It is important to take baby steps and make sure not to use the clicking sound when the cat is too severely stressed. This is because the cat won't be able to direct its attention towards you when tension and stress levels are too high. In this phase and steps, it's all about subtle moments of stress in which the cat feels insecure. Be wary of subtle stress signals, as described in the third chapter.

For example, when your cat walks into the room displaying subtle stress symptoms (such as its whiskers pressed backwards, licking with the tongue, twitching fur, a low-hanging tail), make the clicking sound and wait for a positive response (such as a tail moving upwards, the cat looking up and coming towards you, the cat sitting calmly, closing of the eyes, and so on).

It is important for the cat to first respond positively after hearing the clicking sound, and only rewarding it with a treat once the desired response has been shown.

By doing this phase in this way, you set two processes in motion. On the one hand, in a language it understands, you're saying the following to the cat when it feels insecure: 'Everything is okay. You're allowed to be at ease. You're safe.' And that is truly the case, because you're only allowed to make the clicking sound when there is no danger - visitors, other cats, vacuum cleaner, comb, and so on - around.

On the other hand, the cat learns that when it feels uneasy and you make the clicking sound, it is completely safe in the situation. Because this calms the cat, it is more receptive to become conscious of its environment and the fact that its environment is both in order and safe.
As a result, the clicking sound starts to function as a command. In a more advanced training scenario, this isn't what we'd be looking for, but it's okay for this straightforward technique.

Step 4 - Teaching your cat that the perceived danger is okay.

This is an advanced step, and not everybody has to go this far. Here, you will be telling the cat that although what it's observing may effectively appear a little scary and dangerous (visitors, another cat, a new sofa, and so on), it's actually completely fine and not dangerous at all.

The cat will uneasily come closer to observe. You then make the clicking sound, wait for a positive behavioural change and give the cat a treat, like in the previous step. Here, it is also very important that the scary situation or stimulus isn't too invasive (in other words, too strong)! You will never be able to sell a dog or a toddler walking towards the cat or a party full of people as 'okay' or 'safe' in this way. Your cat will never be at ease in those situations.

Therefore, start with scripted situations, like, for example, having a friend over whom you've asked to ignore the cat so that you can employ the technique. If this goes well over multiple times, next time ask your friend to softly talk to the cat while you use the technique. In this way, you can gradually build up; from talking to the cat, to calmly sticking out a hand and allowing the cat to sniff it, briefly touching the cat, playing, and so on. Make sure that you also take tiny steps and gradually build them up here!

This gives your cat the chance to grow and experience success. By implementing this technique, the cat will become more resilient and also develop a better and more secure feeling in relation to its environment, and all the triggers and stimuli in it, outside of training sessions.
Good luck!

Afterword from the author

The book is finally done. I'd like to express few final thoughts here.

I hope I've inspired you to start viewing your cat from a different perspective. Not distressed or panicky, but with more confidence and enthusiasm to improve both your cat's and your own happiness. Because that's what it's all about.

Since the start of my career (and I have had the good fortune of being able to start at an early age), cats have fascinated me tremendously.

Specifically, how it is possible for a cat, with all its preprogrammed primitive instincts, to succeed within our artificial human environment and blossom into the most popular pet of the twenty-first century. The videos on YouTube don't lie. What attracts us so to cats?

Perhaps we want to be more like cats? Elegant, independent, determined, indifferent, opportunistic, living in the moment and enjoying it? Without wanting to change a thing? Being content with what we've got and not fretting the small stuff too much?

For me, without a doubt, cats are soul mates. Teachers who, through their behaviour, teach me what is important and show me what to do to get closer to myself.

Animals are mirrors; they reflect our deep-rooted emotions and desires.

What can we learn from them? To always be ready to play, no matter how silly or seemingly small the opportunity. To not allow ourselves to be influenced by what others think of us.

To adopt a no-nonsense attitude towards those things which deep down aren't important for us and to not make a fuss about them.

Their incredible adaptability to their environment and flexibility (both physically and mentally) can stimulate us to spend more time on our own well-being. To give attention to a healthy eating pattern, plenty of movement, and to play, play, and play some more. To rest plenty and to enjoy moments in the sun.

Cats are born entrepreneurs with their infectious desire to explore each and every day. They teach us it is okay to strive for what you believe in and what you desire.

A lot of the theory about the mental, physical and emotional well-being of animals is directly applicable to people. And I meet a lot of cat lovers who use the info they obtain about their cat in their own lives and become happier people themselves as a result.

I hope this book will contribute towards developing an optimal relationship with your cat and all cats that you will ever welcome into your now perfectly adapted home.

With love, Anneleen

About the author

Anneleen Bru (1985) adopted her first cat, Madeleine, a Birman, when she was 17. Little did she know this would be the start of a spectacular adventure. When the time came to choose the topic of her thesis for the university programme Communication Sciences at Antwerp University, she chose the topic 'communication among cats' and, in this way, became conscious of the fact that a considerable number of cats end up in shelters due to hidden behavioural problems every year.

This is how Anneleen ended up in Southampton (UK), where she completed the three-year Master's programme Companion Animal Behaviour Counselling, thus becoming the first non-veterinary, cat behavioural therapist, university graduate in Flanders, Belgium.

Things shifted into another gear in 2008 with the launch of Felinova; consultations were quickly followed by lectures and training programmes about cat behaviour for enthusiasts and professionals alike. Often heard feedback is: 'She is able to explain things in an interesting way, with passion, and lots of humour.' People are on the edge of their seats when Anneleen starts talking, and she quickly learnt that this is the best way to reach cat owners about the well-being of their cat and to convince them to treat their cats differently.

Besides domestic cats, Anneleen also ended up in Kenya to assist with a study into social behaviour among giraffes. By giving a lecture about training giraffes at an international giraffe conference in San Francisco, she found herself entering the world of zoos. Here, she works together intensively with animal carers and their beautiful animals, which so far has included lions, mandrills, bongos, tapirs, hippos, giraffes, North American porcupines, jaguars, Amur leopards, red ruffed lemurs and spider

monkeys. As a result of this adventure, she was part of the television programme 'De Zoo achter de schermen' on BVN for two seasons.
Anneleen is regularly invited to appear as a cat expert on a wide range of television and radio programmes, and writes her cat column for Story, among others.

In addition to behavioural modification among animals, Anneleen's other great passion is bringing people together and coaching them to further expand this new sector. Her famous cat conference 'Poes Café' (translation is 'Cat Coffee', a *French reference name for an after-dinner liqueur, here referring to a get-together to talk and learn about cats*), which is held annually in November, was held for the fifth time in 2017 and had twice as many participants as in previous years. Cat lovers and professionals come from far and wide to hear national and international speakers talk about cat behaviour and well-being. In 2015, she launched the Felinova Cat Coach © Diploma. An intensive vocational programme for professionals working with cats and who want to master all facets of the cat to better assist their customers. We're going into its third year, and at present, the programme already has 25 graduates. After all, 'together we stand strong' is Anneleen's deepest conviction.

And now the ultimate dream - the first book - has become a reality. With this book, Anneleen hopes to reach more people to increase their understanding of cat behaviour and by doing so give cats a better life.